SEAFOOD COOKBOOK

Re-imagine Seafood With Delicious and Unique Catfish Recipes

(Become a Seafood Expert With Seafood Recipes)

Carmen Robinson

Published by Alex Howard

© **Carmen Robinson**

All Rights Reserved

Seafood Cookbook: Re-imagine Seafood With Delicious and Unique Catfish Recipes (Become a Seafood Expert With Seafood Recipes)

ISBN 978-1-990169-84-7

All rights reserved. No part of this guide may be reproduced in any form without permission in writing from the publisher except in the case of brief quotations embodied in critical articles or reviews.

Legal & Disclaimer

The information contained in this book is not designed to replace or take the place of any form of medicine or professional medical advice. The information in this book has been provided for educational and entertainment purposes only.

The information contained in this book has been compiled from sources deemed reliable, and it is accurate to the best of the Author's knowledge; however, the Author cannot guarantee its accuracy and validity and cannot be held liable for any errors or omissions. Changes are periodically made to this book. You must consult your doctor or get professional medical advice before using any of the suggested remedies, techniques, or information in this book.

Table of contents

Part 1 1

VOLEO'S   CAJUN BARBECUE SHRIMP 2

SAVANNAH SEAFOOD SUPREME 4

SAVANNAH LOW COUNTRY BOIL 8

TITUSVILLE SHRIMP DIAVOLO 11

JACKSONVILLE BEACH   SHRIMP PATE' 13

Simple, sweet and neat 13

KEY WEST SHRIMP FRITTERS 14

RAGIN' SHRIMP CREOLE 15

LOBSTER SAFFRON ENSHELL 18

CREAMED CAYENNE LOBSTER 20

THE BEST LOBSTER SANDWICH 22

OYSTERS EN BROCHETTE' 24

APALACHACOLA KICKIN' BUTT OYSTER CHOWDER 26

VOLEO'S ORIGINAL   OYSTER & ARTICHOKE BISQUE .. 28

TARPON SPRINGS SCALLOPS ENSHELL 30

STUFFED SCALLOPS 32

SCALLOP PIE 34

BAHAMIAN CONCH FRITTERS 38

BAHAMAS CRISPY FRIED CONCH 40

KISSIMMEE RIVER HUSHPUPPIES 42

AUNT BLANCH'S KISSIMMEE CORNBREAD 44

GRANDMA BROWN'S COBBLER 45

BRIAN'S GRILLED CORN 47

Part 2 49

Introduction 50

Crispy Fish and Peppers 51

Cornmeal Crusted Pork 53

Lentil Soup with Beef and Red Pepper 55

White Bean Tuna Salad 57

Cabbage Rolls 59

Lasagna Buns 61

Spinach Pie 62

Chorizo & Sweet Potato Enchiladas 65

Easy White Spinach Pizza 67

Summer Vegetable Tian 69

Roast Chicken with Potatoes and Butternut Squash .. 71

Cauliflower Bake 73

Lightened Up Sesame Chicken 74

Grilled Chicken and Two-Bean Salad 76

Spinach and Egg Sandwiches 77

Farfalle with watercress, cherry tomatoes and feta ... 79

Thai Coconut Shrimp Soup 80

Buddha Stir-Fry 81

Ham & Swiss Sliders 83

Shepherd's Pie Recipe 85

Sweet & Spicy Chicken Wings 87

Baked apples stuffed with dried fruit and pecans 88

Spinach and Potato Breakfast Hash 90

Roasted Cauliflower and Aged White Cheddar Soup.. 93

Creamy Slow Cooker Tortellini Soup 95

Poor Man Husband Casserole 97

Cabbage Noodle Salad 98

Basque Pil Pil Cod 99

Broiled Cajun Swordfish 100

Catfish Creole 101

Coconut Shrimp Patties 102

Guacamole Tuna Wraps 103

Halibut Roll-Ups 104

Hawaiian Salmon Ceviche 106

Honey Garlic Shrimp 107

Horseradish Salmon Patties 108

Jalapeno Snapper 109

Lemon Blackened Bass 110

Lobster Salad 111

Mackerel Dip 112

Marinera Soup 113

Olive Relish Tuna 115

Orange Grilled Swordfish 117

Pork Salmon Cakes... 118

Prosciutto Scallops 119

Red Snapper Mango Ceviche 120

Rosemary Baked Salmon.. 122

Stewed Cod & Capers... 123

Thai Tuna Ceviche 125

Tomato Halibut Stew 126

Tomato Sauce Salmon 127

Tuna Artichokes 128

Tuna Burgers... 129

Tuna Sardine Patties 130

Tunisian Cod 131

Tuscan Cod 133

Wasabi Avocado Crab Cakes 135

20 Minute Hamburger Skillet Stew	137
Antiguan Charcoal Baked Bananas	138
Aunt Sarah's Chili Sauce	139
Australian Grilled Fish	140
Baked Stuffed Fish	141
Best Peach Cobbler	142
Biscuit And Pancake Mix	143
Blackened Fish	144
Blazing Trail Mix	145
Box Oven	146
Buckwheat Pecan Pancakes For Camping	147
Burgers In Foil	148
Buttermilk Biscuits	149
Camp Au Gratin Potatoes	150
Camp Chili	152
Camp Cobbler Delight	153
Camp Hash	154

Camp Pasta 155

Camp Potatoes... 156

Camp Stew 157

Camper's Baked Potatoes 158

Camper's Cookies... 159

Camper's Sausage 160

Camper's Stew 161

Campers Hobo Pie 162

Campers Pizza Pie 163

Campfire Biscuits 164

Campfire Cinnamon Coffeecake............................... 165

Campfire Fondue 166

Campfire Fried Rice.. 167

Campfire Hash 168

Campfire Pork And Beans 169

Dutch Oven Biscuits 170

Dutch Oven Trout 171

Flank Steak Teriyaki 172

Foiled Burgers Aka "Jack Special" 173

Great Outdoors Potatoes 174

Grilled Sausage & Sweet Mustard In Tortillas 175

Homemade Granola 177

Irish Soda Bread 178

Lazy Or "Dump" Cobbler 179

Mountain Man Breakfast 181

Never Fail Dumplings 183

Onioned Potatoes 184

Part 1

VOLEO'S
CAJUN BARBECUE SHRIMP

The Finished Product

Note: there are about 50 ways to make Cajun BBQ Shrimp. However, Voleo's is one of the best. Cajun secret: Fat in the head promotes an exceptional flavor when left on when cooked. However, if you desire, remove the heads before serving. Put heads in a pan cover with water and boil down to ¼ cup. Add to the pan. If your shrimp don't have heads on, make it anyway, but taste will suffer.

INGREDIENTS (SERVES 2)

1 LB SHRIMP (HEADS ON PREFERABLY)

1 TEASPOON BLACK PEPPER (less makes it milder, but 1 is best)

1 TABLESPOON PAUL PRUDHOMME'S SEAFOOD MAGIC*

1 TABLESPOON ROSEMARY, GROUND OR POUNDED (RUBBED)

1 TABLESPOON GRANULATED GARLIC (OR 3 FRESH CLOVES, MINCED)

1 TABLESPOON FRESH CHOPPED PARSLEY

2 TABLESPOONS LEA & PERRIN WORCESHIRE SAUCE

1/4 POUND BUTTER (1 STICK)

1 TABLESPOON CHICKEN BASE IN 1 CUP WATER (BUY IN STORES, IT'S WHAT IS USED IN NEW ORLEANS AND IS MUCH, MUCH BETTER THAN CANNED BROTH)

2 TABLESPOONS BEER

METHOD

Start with a very hot skillet. Place the shrimp in the pan, cover with half the butter and toss. Place the following on top of the shrimp/butter quickly and toss: Seafood magic, pepper, rosemary, garlic and parsley. Pour chicken base around the base and add the Lea &

Perrins and beer over it all and toss. Add the remaining butter, toss and serve. Dig in and peel the shrimp as its 'elbow lickin' good.

SAVANNAH SEAFOOD SUPREME

INGREDIENTS (SERVES 4)

1 POUND SHRIMP DEHEADED, PEELED, DEVEINED AND RESERVED

3 EGG YOLKS, BEATEN AND ADDED TO THE CREAM, SET ASIDE

1 PINT HEAVY CREAM

1/2 STICK BUTTER

1 BUNCH CHIVES or CILANTRO, CHOPPED, SAVE A FEW FOR

GARNISH

2 TABLESPOONS FLOUR

1/2 CUP SHERRY

1/2 TEASPOON NUTMEG

1/2 POUND BLUE CRAB MEAT (two cans)

1 1/2 CUPS COOKED PASTA OR RICE

1 TABLESPOON GROUND ROSEMARY

2 TABLESPOONS BUTTER

METHOD

Peel and de-vein shrimp, set aside

Examine the crab for shell pieces and set aside

Beat the egg yolks in the cream and set aside

Cook the rice or pasta, drain the rice/pasta; add 2 tablespoons butter and the

rosemary. Mix, cover and set aside.

In a pan, heat the butter and sauté the chives/cilantro on medium heat.

While greenery is sautéing, add the flour and cook for about a minute.

Add the sherry, cream & egg yolks, nutmeg and crab meat. Stir and cook to

proper consistency; taste.

Adjust salt & pepper. Meanwhile.

Now, place the shrimp in a butter, black pepper mixture, then remove to the

grill or broiler. Watch closely as they cook very quickly. Turn once and remove when the shrimp turns white or slightly browned by the butter.

Place the shrimp, arranged artistically on top of the sauce/rice or pasta.

Garnish with chives, basil leaves or cilantro leaves.

SAVANNAH BLUES

Once you have experienced Savannah, you will always go back. Savannah, Georgia offers some of the best food in the South. The city squares, the atmosphere and of course the food will make it a time to remember. At night, places like the River Walk, the Pirates House, small seafood houses and wonderful old-world drinking establishments can show Savannah at its best. In addition to the restaurants serving seafood to beef and cooling drinks, the neighborhood cookouts are unique to Savannah. Not your daddy's barbecue grill.

There are two types of basic outdoor parties: The Oyster Roast, and the Low Country Boil. Savannah locals take their oysters seriously. On a Friday or Saturday night, the number of oyster roasts is innumerable. The low country boil is practiced night or day. Both feature not only food, but music and drinks as well.

Low country boil is a favorite of not only Savannah residents but is done all over the south in varying recipes. The students of Georgia Southern often used a low country boil as an excuse to party. This recipe was brought to light by Georgia Southern graduates, Brian Lee. Scott & Machelle Cecil, Paul C. Reddick III, Darius Sojka, Alex Kambar, Pat Cook and also Don & Wanda VanDerRyt, Low country boil is easy to make and has enough variety for all and is a real crowd pleaser.

Everyone at the party gathers around, shucks corn, cuts sausage and washes potatoes, chops onion and peels shrimp, but most just drink beer. Served with drawn butter, good crusty bread and a salad; it is a feast worthy of good friends, good music and good drink. Try a low country boil, and think Savannah, Georgia. The Jewel of the South.

SAVANNAH LOW COUNTRY BOIL

You will need a big pot with a basket, like a turkey fryer
Version # 16, Serves roughly 15 people

INGREDIENTS

1 BOX OLD BAY SEASONING

3 POUNDS SMALL RED POTATOES

5 POUNDS SAUSAGE CUT INTO 3-INCH PIECES (POLISH, SMOKED OR ITALIAN)

12 EARS FRESH SHUCKED CORN, EACH BROKEN INTO 2 PIECES

3 to 6 ONIONS, QUARTERED

16 WHOLE GARLIC BULBS (ABOUT 2 POUNDS)

5 POUNDS SHRIMP WITH SHELLS ON

SALT & PEPPER

METHOD

In enough water to just cover the food, boil the water in the pot.

2. When boiling, place the empty basket back in the water. Add 3/4 cup old bay seasoning to the boiling water.

Add the cut-up sausage and the potatoes and cook for 10 minutes.

Add the corn, onions, garlic and cook for another 4 minutes.

Lastly, add the shrimp, remove from the heat and let stand 5 minutes

Pull the basket out and dump the feast out on newspaper and sprinkle a little more Old Bay Seasoning,

Serve with drawn butter and a salad.

Note: shrimp cooked with the heads on; add a subtle, delightful flavor.

TITUSVILLE SHRIMP DIAVOLO

INGEDIENTS

1 WHOLE GARLIC HEAD

2 STICKS BUTTER

2 POUNDS SHRIMP, HEADS ON PREFERRED

2 TABLESPOONS BLACK PEPPER, COARSE GROUND

FRENCH BREAD (TO EAT WITH THE SHRIMP OR THIN CRISP GARLIC BREAD TO ACCOMPANY EACH BITE)

METHOD

Crush and chop the garlic very fine.

Melt the butter and add the black pepper and garlic, set aside

Skewer 6 to 8 shrimp, shell on. (4 skewers per person)

Grill the shrimp; be careful as they cook very fast

Transfer the shrimp to a serving bowls and cover with the butter mixture.

If the heads are on, pull them off, peel and eat.

Option 1—If shrimp are de-headed that's ok. If they are peeled, that's ok too.

Option 2—If no grill is available, place in a pan, cover raw shrimp with butter sauce and cook until shrimp turn pink.

Note: Some like to place a buttery shrimp on a piece of French bread and bite;

While others like to place a shrimp on a small piece of garlic bread and bite.

JACKSONVILLE BEACH
SHRIMP PATE'
Simple, sweet and neat

INGREDIENTS

2 POUNDS COOKED, PEELED AND DE-VIENED SHRIMP

1 LEMON

YOUR FAVORITE HOT SAUCE

MAYONAISE

GOOD PARTY CRACKERS

METHOD

Chop the shrimp in a blender or food processor.

Add the juice of 1 lemon, just enough mayonnaise to bind, add your favorite

hot sauce to taste. The consistency should be almost dry.

Serve with good party crackers, or with a wig (see story opposite).

KEY WEST SHRIMP FRITTERS
Simple easy crunchers

INGREDIENTS

1/2 POUND SHRIMP, COOKED, SHELLED AND CHOPPED

1 CUP FLOUR

1 TEASPOON BAKING SODA

2 TEASPOONS MINCED GARLIC

1/2 RED BELL PEPPER, CHOPPED

3 SCALLIONS, CHOPPED

1 TEASPOON WORCESHIRE SAUCE

OIL FOR FRYING

HOT SAUCE FOR TASTE

1 CUP BEER OR WATER

OPTION: CHOP ONE RED PEPPER AND ADD TO MIX

METHOD

Mix all ingredients with beer to a slightly pouring consistency.

Let stand covered for 1 hour. Fry between 300 and 360 degrees in small batches.

Dip large spoons full into hot oil.

Turn once. Serve as an appetizer or accompaniment.

RAGIN' SHRIMP CREOLE
Top Secret recipe by the 'Agin' Cajun

South Lafitte, LA.

NOTE: This recipe is a little complex, but the final product is worth the effort and you will have sufficient to freeze for other times. Half the sauce serves roughly 4 to 6 with 3 pounds shrimp. Button popping good I guarantee!

INGREDIENTS
Cajun Power Sauces make this recipe

3 POUNDS SHRIMP, PEELED AND DEVEINED
6 RIBS CELERY CHOPPED
2 RED AND 2 YELLOW ONIONS DICED SMALL
1 RED, 1 YELLOW AND 1 GREEN BELL PEPPER, DICED SMALL
8 CLOVES GARLIC MINCED
1 STICK BUTTER
1 RED, YELLOW AND GREEN BELL PEPPER MINCED FINE
1/2 CUP OLIVE OIL
2 QUARTS SHRIMP STOCK (SEE BELOW)
1 BOTTLE CLAM JUICE
4 STANDARD CANS STEWED TOMATOES
3 6-OZ. CANS TOMATO PASTE

1-QUART KETCHUP

ADD 1/2 TEASPOON WHITE AND BLACK PEPPER (TOTAL 1 TEASPOON)

ADD 2 TABLESPOONS <u>CAJUN POWER CREOLE SEASONING</u> (ADDRESS BELOW)

5 TABLESPOONS <u>CAJUN POWER TIGER SAUCE</u>

1 TABLESPOON <u>CAJUN POWER GARLIC SAUCE</u>

ADD 7 TABLESPOONS BROWN SUGAR

2 TEASPOONS TEXAS PETE OR SIMILAR HOT SAUCE

ADD 3 TABLESPOONS WORCESTERSHIRE SAUCE

2 TEASPOONS SALT

4 TEASPOONS CHOPPED FRESH THYME OR 1 ½ TEASPOONS DRIED THYME

1/4 CUP FRESH SQUEEZED LEMON JUICE

3/4 CUP WHITE WINE

COOKED RICE FOR THE NUMBER YOU INTEND TO FEED TO PUT UNDER THE CREOLE

METHOD

Shrimp stock: Peel and devein shrimp and set aside. Reserve heads and shells.

Add 2-1/4 quarts water and bring to a boil. Add 2 tablespoons chopped onion, celery tops, 1 carrot chopped fine, 3 bay leaves and 5 peppercorns. Simmer and strain. This makes 2 cups stock.

Sauté all the veggies in olive oil until tender. Add all the other ingredients except the shrimp. Simmer for 90 to 120 minutes. Note: this recipe makes a lot of sauce, so freeze what you do not intend to use now (not the shrimp).

Important: Turn off heat and add shrimp to the pot and let stand 2 to 5 minutes.

This will cook the shrimp which will be very tender but not overcooked.

Serve over 1 cup rice, and garnish with fresh chopped parsley.

Once tried, you'll never be satisfied with any other Shrimp Creole.

LOBSTER SAFFRON ENSHELL

INGREDIENTS (SERVES 2)

2 FLORIDA LOBSTER TAILS

1/2 TEASPOON SAFFRON

1/4 CUP MINCED ONION

4 TABLESPOONS WHITE WINE

4 TABLESPOONS WHITE WINE VINEGAR

1/4 CUP HEAVY CREAM

2 STICKS COLD BUTTER, CUT INTO TABLESPOON SIZE PIECES.

SALT, WHITE PEPPER

METHOD

In a Heavy saucepan, place the saffron, onion, vinegar and white wine and bring to a boil. Simmer and reduce to about 4 tablespoons.

Reduce the cream in another pan to about 4 tablespoons.

Add the cream to the first pan with all ingredients, reduce heat to simmer

Add the butter, one piece at a time. (Be very careful not to overheat or it will liquefy).

Remove and season with salt and white pepper, set aside.

Remove lobster meat from the shell, reserving the shell intact. Steam the shells briefly until they turn red.

Split the lobster tail and poach in ½ cup water.

Remove the lobster and slice into ½ inch pieces. Reduce the poaching water to 1 tablespoon.

Replace the lobster back in the shell.

Add the cooled, poaching water to the sauce and top the lobster with the Saffron sauce.

Serve with sliced avocado and mango slices.

CREAMED CAYENNE LOBSTER

INGREDIENTS (Serves 2)

2 FLORIDA LOBSTERS, RAW IF POSSIBLE (NOT PRE-COOKED)

3 TABLESPOONS BUTTER

1 RIPE RED BELL PEPPER

1 ONION

1/4 TEASPOON CAYENNE

1/2 CUP HEAVY CREAM

2 TABLESPOONS CHOPPED FRESH PARSLEY

FETTUCCINE FOR 2

1 LARGE AVACODO OR 2 SMALL

METHOD

Cook the pasta to al dente, drain and set aside.

Using shears or a serrated knife, cut the bottom sides of the shell, peel the bottom off. Using a knife, loosen the raw lobster tail and remove the meat.

Split the lobster and chop into small pieces and set aside.

In a sauce pan, heat the butter and sauté the red bell pepper, onion and cayenne over medium heat.

When the bell pepper has softened, stir in the cream, parsley and salt to taste. Cook until it thickens to a sauce consistency.

Add the lobster and set off the stove with lid on for 5 minutes. This will cook the lobster and keep it tender.

Serve the sauce over the pasta. Top the dish with avocado balls and sliced tomatoes. Serve with a Cesar salad and side dish.

The Real Hidden Harbor at Hidden

THE BEST LOBSTER SANDWICH

INGREDIENTS

2 SLIGHTLY STEAMED LOBSTER

A GOOD DELI BREAD OR ROLL SLICED IN 3 PIECES

8 SLICES BACON COOKED, SLOW AND CRISP

1 LARGE RED RIPE TOMATO, SLICED THIN

LEAF, BIB OR ENDIVE LETTUCE

MAYONNAISE

HOT SAUCE OF YOUR CHOICE

METHOD

Remove the lobster from the shell and slice thin.

Mix your favorite hot sauce in the mayo to taste

Spread the mayo mix on the bottom piece of bread

Place a layer of lobster, a layer of tomato, a layer of bacon.

Spread the mayo mix on the middle piece of bread, both sides.

Place on top of the bacon.

Layer the lobster, tomato and bacon again and complete the sandwich with

the top bun with mayo mix on it.

Slice the sandwich in half and serve with plantain chips or something else crunchy.

OYSTERS EN BROCHETTE'
NEW ORLEANS, LOUISIANNA

As best remembered

INGREDIENTS (SERVES 4)

36 SHUCKED OYSTERS (9 PER PERSON)

3 LEMONS

BEER BATTER

2 CUPS FLOUR

18 STRIPS BACON

12 WOODEN SKEWERS

1 CUP FLOUR AND ENOUGH BEER FOR A THIN BATTER

SALT & PEPPER

OIL

METHOD

Add some salt and pepper to the flour.

Divide the flour in to 2 separate shallow containers. In the first one, place 1 cup seasoned flour.

In the second one, the other cup seasoned flour.

Add enough beer in the bowl flour to make a thin batter.

Add 2 tablespoons oil. The flour in the second container is to roll the battered product in before frying.

Half cook the bacon and cut the strips in half.

Skewer one end of the bacon, skewer the oyster then the other end of the bacon, so it wraps around the oyster.

Put 3 on a skewer and dip them in the batter. Roll the battered skewered oyster in the dry flour and place them in a deep fryer.

Fry at 350 degrees.

Remove from the fryer and immediately squeeze fresh lemon juice over the Oysters En Brochette. Serve immediately.

APALACHACOLA KICKIN' BUTT OYSTER CHOWDER

INGREDIENTS

1-1/2 STICKS BUTTER

6 STALKS CELERY, FINELY CHOPPED

3 LARGE ONIONS, CHOPPED

5 LARGE DICED, BARELY TENDER, COOKED POTATOES

6 COOKED CARROTS, DICED

2 QUARTS FRESH SHUCKED OYSTERS WITH OYSTER LIQUID

4 CUPS HALF & HALF

2 CUPS WHOLE MILK

1/2 CUP VODKA (THE SECRET INGREDIENT)

4 TABLESPOONS DRIED SAGE

2 TEASPOONS FRESH PARSLEY

3 TEASPOONS CELERY SEED

3 TABLESPOONS WORCESTERSHIRE SAUCE

TABASCO SAUCE TO TASTE

FRESHLEY GROUND SALT & PEPPER

METHOD

Melt ½ stick butter in a large pot over medium heat.

Add the celery and onion and sauté until the onion is translucent.

Add the par-boiled potatoes and carrots to the mix; heat and toss.

Drain liquor from the oysters and reserve.

Add oysters to the veggie mix and cook until the edges of the oysters begin

to curl.

Add all of the remaining ingredients including the oyster liquor. Stir and bring the chowder to just below simmer.

Melt the remaining butter and add. Stir and season with salt and fresh ground black pepper.

Serve immediately with crackers and get out of the way as your guests will make total pigs of themselves. This is one oyster chowder that is definitely 'Kickin' Butt Good'!

VOLEO'S ORIGINAL
OYSTER & ARTICHOKE BISQUE

Rich and Creamy Seafood Bisque

INGREDIENTS

1/3 LB UNSALTED BUTTER

2 CUPS FLOUR

2 8-OZ CANS ARTICHOKES, CHOPPED & DRAINED (SAVE THE JUICE)

2 CANS CHICKEN BASE (NOT BROTH)

1 QUART CHOPPED OYSTERS

1 QUART HEAVY CREAM

1 QUART HALF & HALF

3 TABLESPOONS BLACK PEPPER

3 TABLESPOONS GARLIC POWDER

3 TABLESPOONS RED PEPPER FLAKES

2 TABLESPOONS CAJUN SEASONING (ITL)

2 TABLESPOONS VEGGIE-MAGIC SEASONING

METHOD

Make a roux with the butter and flour.

Add the finely chopped artichokes.

Drain oysters and mix oyster juice with the artichoke juice and chicken base. If needed, add enough liquid to make ½ gallon liquid.

Chop the oysters and set aside.

Add the liquid to the roux. Add the cream and half & half. Add the seasonings. When almost boiling, add the oysters and simmer just a little. NOTE: Chicken base is not broth. It is a richer, saltier chicken seasoning used by restaurants and is sold in most grocery chains.

TARPON SPRINGS SCALLOPS ENSHELL

A Typical Serving (with other side dishes) and Salad

INGREDIENTS (SERVES 2)

BAY OR CALICO SCALLOPS ARE PREFERRED, BUT YOU CAN USE THE LARGER SEA SCALLOPS CUT INTO PIECES. A TYPICAL SERVING OF BAY OR CALICO SCALLOPS IS 18 TO 24 PER PERSON OR A HALF DOZEN AS AN APPETIZER.

48 BAY SCALLOPS WITH SHELLS OR OTHER CONTAINERS

6–8 GARLIC CLOVES, CRUSHED & CHOPPED FINE

1 STICK OF BUTTER

1 CUP OF VERY COARSE BREAD CRUMBS (PANCO WILL DO NICELY) OR MAKE YOUR OWN.

METHOD

Place the scallops in shells or bowls, on a cookie sheet or broiler pan.

Crush & chop the garlic, add the butter and microwave till butter is melted.

Place the scallops in the shells or other container

Place the garlic and butter, evenly distributed, on the scallops

Top with coarse bread crumbs

Broil until the crumbs brown.

The scallops will be done and tender.

Use a spoon and scoop out the garlic-butter-scallop-bread crumbs.

STUFFED SCALLOPS

INGREDIENTS

1 CUP CHOPPED SCALLOPS

1/2 BELL PEPPER, FINELY CHOPPED

1/2 ONION, FINELY CHOPPED

4 SLICES BACON, COOKED CRISP

1-1/4 CUPS SEASONED STUFFING

1 EGG, BEATEN

1/2 TEASPOON THYME

1/2 TEASPOON SALT

2 TABLESPOON MILK OR HALF & HALF

1 TEASPOON RED PEPPER FLAKES (OPTIONAL)

METHOD

Cook stove stop stuffing per directions.

Cook the bacon crisp, then crumble.

Sauté bell pepper and onion in bacon fat and drain.

Mix all ingredients except half the bacon and only one cup of the stuffing.

Spoon the mixture into the shells.

Top with the remaining crushed season stuffing and remaining bacon.

Bake at 375 degrees until browned.

SCALLOP PIE

INGREDIENTS

1/2 CUP MILK

1/2 CUP FLOUR

1/2 STICK BUTTER PLUS 2 TABLESPOONS

1/2 POUND SCALLOPS

1 TEASPOON BAKING POWDER

2 GARLIC CLOVES, MINCED

1/2 CUP CHICKEN STOCK

8 OUNCES RICOTTA CHEESE

1/2 MEDIUM ONION, MINCED

1/4 CUP SHERRY

1 TEASPOON SALT

METHOD

In the baking dish, melt the ½ stick butter in the oven at 350 degrees.

Take the baking dish with the melted butter out and set aside.

Mix the milk, flour, baking powder and salt. (this is the batter)

In a saucepan, sauté the onions and garlic in 2 tablespoons butter; when

done, add the scallops and cook until white (1 to 2 minutes).

Add the chicken stock, cheese and sherry, mix 1 minute over low heat

Pour the batter evenly into the baking dish with the butter.

Pour the filling evenly on top of the batter, do not stir.

Place the baking dish back into a 350-degree oven for about 20 minutes or

until the top browns.

Note: the batter will naturally rise to the top and brown nicely.

SCALLOPS MEDITERRANEAN

INGREDIENTS

1 LARGE EGGPLANT

6 CLOVES GARLIC + 2 MORE (8)

OLIVE OIL

OREGANO

4 TABLESPOONS BUTTER

PANKO BREAD CRUMBS

1 POUND BAY, CALICO or SEA SCALLOPS

1 TABLESPOON SAFFRON

1/2 CUP CHICKEN STOCK

1-1/2 CUPS HEAVY CREAM

SALT AND PEPPER

METHOD

Slice the eggplant crossways into 3/8-inch-thick rounds; peel. Salt each slice liberally and stand on edge in a bowl for an hour to draw the moisture out. Rinse the salt off and pat dry.

Crush 6 cloves garlic. Cover eggplant with olive oil on each side, place in a baking pan and top with 4 cloves garlic. Sprinkle with oregano and bake at 300 degrees until browned.

In a sauce pan, sauté the scallops in 4 tablespoons butter and the 2 crushed garlic cloves (chopped). Place equal portions of scallops on each eggplant slice, top with Panko crumbs. Broil until browned.

SAUCE

Soak 2 tablespoons saffron in 1/2 cup hot chicken broth for 30 minutes to infuse the saffron into the broth. Add this to the heavy cream and reduce by one third. Pour around the eggplant. Serve with a side dish and a salad.

BAHAMIAN CONCH FRITTERS

INGREDIENTS

1 POUND CONCH

1/2 LARGE ONION, CHOPPED

1/2 BELL PEPPER, CHOPPED

1 TEASPOON SALT

1 TEASPOON BLACK PEPPER

2 LARGE GARLIC CLOVES, MINCED

1 TEASPOON BAKING POWDER

1 TEASPOON THYME

1/2 CUP FLOUR

1/4 CUP CORN MEAL

1 BEATEN EGG

2 TABLESPOONS OIL FOR THE BATTER

BEER

METHOD

Peel and pound the conch to tenderize, then coarse grind or chop.

In a bowl, place all the dry ingredients, conch and veggies.

In another bowl, pour in 2 tablespoons beer, add the egg and oil. Beat together. Add to the bowl of dry ingredients, conch and veggies.

Add enough beer to form a semi-stiff batter.

Spoon the batter into a deep fryer with peanut oil at 300 to 350 degrees. Adjust heat to the amount of fritters in the oil. Fritter batter will cool the oil, you must keep at least 300 degrees for proper cooking.

BAHAMAS CRISPY FRIED CONCH

RECIPE (SERVES 4)

6 to 8 HAND SIZED PIECES OF CONCH, ABOUT A POUND

1-1/2 CUPS SELF RISING (ALL PURPOSE) FLOUR DIVIDED INTO 2 BOWLS

1/2 CUP COARSE HOMEMADE BREAD CRUMBS OR PANKO BREAD CRUMBS

SALT AND PEPPER

1 TABLESPOON BAKING POWDER

BEER, TASTED OF COURSE TO DETERMINE THE QUALITY.

DEEP FRYER OR DEEP OIL IN AN IRON SKILLET

PEANUT OIL (BEST) FOR FRYING

METHOD

Peel the conch with a very sharp knife.

Pound the conch meat with a mallet to break the meat down (tenderize) but do not wreck or tear the meat. Slice the pounded conch into 1-inch strips.

Season both bowls of flour with salt and pepper

In one of the bowls, add 2 tablespoons oil, the baking powder and enough beer to form a thin batter that will adhere to the conch meat.

Add the bread crumbs to the second container of flour.

Heat the oil to 300–350 degrees. Dip the strips into the batter, and then roll them in the second container of dry mix seasoned flour and bread crumbs. Drop them in the oil. They will float to the surface. Remove and drain on paper towels or newspaper when lightly browned.

Note: Conch freezes well with the skin on. It has been known to keep and appear as fresh after several years.

KISSIMMEE RIVER HUSHPUPPIES

Clarence and Cathy White Dipping Hushpuppies

INGREDIENTS

1/2 CUP CORN MEAL

1/2 CUP FLOUR

1 TABLESPOON BAKING POWDER

1/2 TEASPOON SALT

1/4 CUP OIL

1 EGG

1 TABLESPOON BLACK PEPPER

1 MEDIUM ONION, FINELY CHOPPED

1/2 RED BELL PEPPER, MINCED

1 JALAPENO PEPPER, MINCED (OR MORE TO TASTE)

BEER

METHOD

Mix all the dry ingredients thoroughly.

Add the egg that has been beaten in the oil. Mix and add the beer.

In a deep skillet or deep fryer use enough oil to cover the puppies.

Bring the temperature up to 300 to 350 degrees.

Drop in spoon full's of batter. When the bottom browns, turn them over.

Test the first ones the make certain they are cooked; if done, lower the heat.

AUNT BLANCH'S KISSIMMEE CORNBREAD

This recipe has been well traveled and handed down through the generations. It never fails.

INGREDIENTS

2 CUPS BUTTERMILK

2 EGGS

1 TEASPOON SALT

1 TEASPOON BAKING SODA

1 CUP ALL PURPOSE FLOUR

2 CUPS CORNMEAL

4 TABLESPOONS BACON FAT

METHOD

Heat a 10-inch iron fry pan with a little of the bacon fat left in the pan from cooking the bacon. Heat the pan until smoking hot.

Mix together the eggs, salt, soda and buttermilk. Add the flour, cornmeal and bacon grease.

Carefully pour the batter into the skillet and bake at 450 degrees or until the top is lightly golden.

Slather the slices with creamy butter and homemade jam. Aunt Blanch is still with us in her food.

GRANDMA BROWN'S COBBLER

INGREDIENTS

3 CUPS GUAVAS, BERRIES, PEACHES OR OTHER FRUIT WORKS WELL USE HALF THE AMOUNT OF FRUIT FOR JAPENESE PLUMBS. IF CANNED USE ALL THE JUICE IN THE CAN (2 CANS WORK WELL)

1/2 CUP FLOUR

1/2 CUP MILK

1/2 CUP SUGAR

1/2 STICK BUTTER

1 TEASPOON BAKING SODA

1/4 TEASPOON SALT

METHOD

In a mixing bowl, put in all the ingredients except the butter. This makes the batter.

In a baking dish, put in the butter. Place the baking dish and butter in the oven until the butter is melted.

Remove and pour in the batter evenly over the butter. Then pour in the fruit evenly over the batter.

Place in the oven and bake about 15 to 20 minutes until the batter covers and browns.

For a sweet topping, mix an additional 2 tablespoons cold butter, 2 ½ tablespoons flour, 2 tablespoons sugar and 1 tablespoon cinnamon. Cut the butter into the mix until crumbly. When the top of the cobbler begins to brown; sprinkle the topping over the crust of the cobbler. Continue baking until crisp (about 10 minutes.). Ice cream or heavy cream is an optional accompaniment.

BRIAN'S GRILLED CORN
WITH GARLIC ROSEMARY BUTTER

INGREDIENTS

(SERVES 10 AS A SIDE DISH)

5 LARGE EARS CORN

1 STICK BUTTER

6 LARGE CLOVES GARLIC

2 TABLESPOONS GROUND ROSEMARY

ONE HOT GRILL

METHOD

Shuck the corn, removing the entire tassel.

Smash and chop the garlic very fine

Grind enough rosemary to make 2 tablespoons

In a small pot, place 1 stick of butter, the garlic and rosemary.

Heat until the butter begins to bubble.

With a small brush or mop, brush the corn and place on the grill over open flame. Turn 4 times, browning as you turn.

Cut the corn in 2 pieces and roll in the hot butter mixture as you serve it. Once you try this, you won't go back to just butter.

Part 2

Introduction

Thank you for downloading my Meals on a Budget Recipe book! Doctors and nutritionist advise that we should eat vegetables and fruits everyday but for some people this can be next to impossible if they have very low monthly incomes

In this cookbook, there are recipes that you can easily prepare at home inexpensively, you will be surprised at how budget friendly these recipes are. Enjoy!

Crispy Fish and Peppers

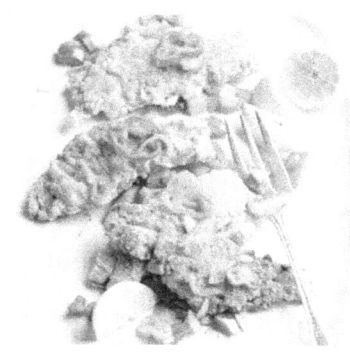

Ingredients
- 1 pound fresh or frozen (thawed) small fish fillets (such as grouper, catfish, or tilapia)
- ¾ cup buttermilk
- 1 egg
- 1 teaspoon Cajun seasoning
- 1 cup all-purpose flour
- 3 tablespoons vegetable oil
- 1 cup sliced and/or chopped miniature sweet peppers
- 1 lemon, cut up

Directions
- Rinse fish and pat dry with paper towels.

- In a shallow dish, whisk together buttermilk, egg, and Cajun seasoning. Place flour in another shallow dish. Dip fish in buttermilk and flour. Repeat to coat fish twice.
- Heat 3 tablespoons of the oil in a large heavy skillet over medium-high heat. Carefully add fish to hot oil (working in batches, if necessary). Cook for 3 to 5 minutes on each side or until golden. Add more oil, if needed. Drain on paper towels.
- Drain oil from skillet; wipe clean with paper towel. Add peppers to skillet and cook 2 minutes or until crisp tender.
- Serve fish with peppers and lemon.

Cornmeal Crusted Pork

Ingredients
- ½ cup yellow cornmeal
- ½ teaspoon salt
- ½ teaspoon ground black pepper
- 1 egg, lightly beaten
- 1 tablespoon water
- 1 pound pork tenderloin, cut in 1/2-inch thick slices
- 2 tablespoons olive oil or cooking oil
- 12 ounces fresh green beans
- 2 medium zucchini and/or yellow summer squash, thinly bias-sliced
- 2 tablespoons fresh oregano leaves

Directions
- In a shallow dish combine cornmeal, salt and pepper. In another shallow dish combine egg and

water. Dip pork in egg mixture and then in cornmeal mixture to coat.
- Heat oil in a very large skillet over medium-high heat. Add pork and cook 2 minutes per side or until no pink remains.
- Remove to serving platter. Add beans and zucchini to skillet; cook and stir 6 to 8 minutes or until crisp-tender. Add salt and pepper to taste; toss.
- Serve along side pork. Sprinkle with oregano leaves.

Lentil Soup with Beef and Red Pepper

Ingredients
- 1 pound boneless beef sirloin steak
- 4 cups reduced-sodium beef broth
- 1 cup French lentils, rinsed and drained
- 1 cup water
- ¾ cup coarsely chopped red sweet pepper (1 medium)
- ½ cup chopped onion (1 medium)
- ½ cup sliced carrot (1 medium)
- ½ cup sliced celery (1 stalk)
- 2 cloves garlic, minced
- 1 teaspoon ground cumin
- ¼ teaspoon cayenne pepper
- 1/3 cup snipped fresh parsley

Directions

- Trim fat from meat. Cut meat into 3/4-inch pieces. If desired, in a nonstick skillet cook beef over medium-high heat until browned on all sides.
- Place meat in a 3 1/2- or 4-quart slow cooker. Stir in broth, lentils, water, sweet pepper, onion, carrot, celery, garlic, cumin, and cayenne pepper.
- Cover and cook on low-heat setting for 7 to 8 hours or on high-heat setting for 3 1/2 to 4 hours. Stir in parsley. Ladle soup into bowls.

White Bean Tuna Salad

Ingredients
- 1 15 ounce can cannellini beans, rinsed and drained
- 2 5 ounce cans tuna packed in water, drained
- 2 cups lightly packed arugula or spinach
- ½ small red onion, thinly sliced
- ¼ cup fresh flat-leaf Italian parsley, chopped
- ¼ cup red wine vinegar
- 3 tablespoons extra virgin olive oil
- ½ teaspoon dried leaf oregano, crushed
- ¼ teaspoon salt
- ¼ teaspoon ground black pepper
- ½ lemon
- Crusty bread, sliced and toasted (optional)

Directions

- In a large bowl combine beans, tuna, arugula, red onion, and parsley.
- For dressing, in a screw-top jar combine vinegar, oil, oregano, salt, and pepper. Shake well to combine.
- Pour dressing over tuna mixture; toss gently to combine. Squeeze juice from half of a lemon over salad. Serve with toasted crusty bread, if desired.

Cabbage Rolls

Ingredients
- 2 cups uncooked long grain rice
- 1 tablespoon olive oil
- 1/2 medium onion, finely diced
- 1 clove garlic, finely minced
- 1/2 pound hamburger
- salt and pepper
- 1 head of green cabbage
- 1 can tomato sauce

Directions
- Cook the rice according to package instructions.
- Bring a large pot of salted water to a boil. Remove the core of the cabbage with a sharp knife and remove any damages outer leaves. Add the head of cabbage to the boiling water. Once the leaves start

to soften, use tongs to gently peel away the leaves, trying hard to keep each leaf whole. Blanch cabbage for about 5 minutes until leaves start to soften. Remove cabbage from the heat and strain in a colander.

- To make the filling add olive oil to a large frying pan. Saute onion over medium high heat about 5 minutes, add garlic and cook for about 1 minute. Add the hamburger and cook until brown. Salt and pepper to taste.
- Remove from heat and mix hamburger mixture with cooked rice in a large bowl. The key to this dish is to really add flavor with salt and a generous amount of pepper to taste– don't undo this step or you will have bland cabbage rolls.
- Once the cabbage leaves are cool you can add the filling. Use as many of the cabbage leaves as possible until you get to the center of the head of cabbage, where the leaves are white and too small to use. If desired, you can carefully cut away the large center vein from each leaf. Spoon the filling into each leaf. Place the rolls touching each other into a 9" x 13" casserole dish. Pour the can of tomato sauce over the top.
- Cover tightly with foil. Place in a 325 degree oven for 2 hours or 300 degrees for 3 hours.

Lasagna Buns

Ingredients

- 6 sub rolls or bolillo rolls
- About 2 cups spaghetti sauce with meat
- 1/2 cup sour cream (use 1/2 cup ricotta if you prefer)
- 1 egg white
- 1 tsp Italian seasoning
- 1/2 tsp salt
- 2 cup mozzarella cheese, divided
- 1/4 cup Parmesan cheese
- Lettuce, vinaigrette

Directions

- Preheat oven to 350.
- Slice off the tops of the sub rolls. Then scoop out the bread from the inside. Spoon some spaghetti sauce into the rolls.
- In a mixing bowl, combine the sour cream, egg white, spices, salt and 1 cup of the mozzarella cheese. Spoon over the spaghetti sauce.
- Sprinkle a little Parmesan cheese and mozzarella cheese over top. Add the bread top back on. Place into a foil pouch and bake for 25-30 minutes.
- Prepare small, simple side salad.
    - Serve Lasagna Buns with side salad.

Spinach Pie

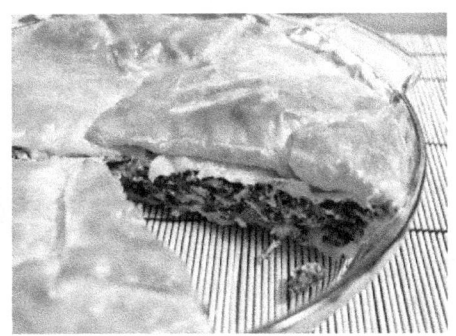

Ingredients

- 1 Tbsp olive oil
- 1 small yellow onion
- 1 clove garlic
- 1 cup cottage cheese
- ¼ cup parmesan cheese
- ⅛ tsp ground nutmeg
- ½ tsp salt
- 10-15 cranks fresh cracked pepper
- 2 large eggs
- 16 oz. frozen cut spinach
- 1 sheet (8 oz.) puff pastry
- 2 Tbsp flour for dusting
- 1 large egg (for glaze, optional)

Directions

- Preheat the oven to 375 degrees. Dice the onion into small pieces and mince the garlic. Cook both in a small skillet with 1 tablespoon of olive oil over medium heat until soft and transparent (about five minutes).
- While the onions and garlic are cooking, prepare the rest of the filling. In a bowl combine the cottage cheese, parmesan cheese, eggs, salt, pepper, and nutmeg. Mix well. Before adding the spinach, strain it in a colander and press out as much moisture as possible (squeezing handfuls in a fist works well too).
- Once the onions have softened, add them to the cheese/egg mixture along with the squeeze dried spinach. Stir until well combined.
- Dust a clean work surface with flour and unfold a sheet of puff pastry onto it. Using a rolling pin, roll the puff pastry into a 12 inch by 12 inch square. Drape the rolled dough over a standard 9 inch pie dish.
- Spread the spinach filling evenly inside the pastry lined pie dish. Fold the corners of the pastry back over top of the filling. It's okay if they do not fully reach to meet each other. If desired, brush a whisked egg over the top (this will give the surface a glossy appearance after cooking).

- Bake the pie for 45 minutes in a preheated 375 degree oven. Allow the pie to rest for about 5 minutes before cutting to allow the filling to set.

Chorizo & Sweet Potato Enchiladas

Ingredients
- 2 Tbsp vegetable oil
- 1 medium (1 lb.) sweet potato
- 1 medium poblano pepper
- 2 cloves garlic
- 3 links (3/4 lb.) chorizo
- 10 taco size tortillas
- 1 (15 oz.) can enchilada sauce
- 1½ cups shredded cheese

Directions
- Peel the sweet potato and cut into a half inch cubes. Remove the stem and seeds from the poblano and also dice into half inch pieces. Mince the garlic.
- In a large skillet, cook the sweet potato, poblano and garlic in vegetable oil, over medium heat until they begin to soften (about 10 minutes). Squeeze the chorizo out of it's casing into the skillet. Break

- up the meat and cook until thoroughly browned (about 5 minutes).
- Spray a large casserole dish with non-stick spray and preheat the oven to 375 degrees. Scoop about ¾ cup of the chorizo sweet potato filling into each tortilla. Fold in the ends and then roll the tortilla up around the filling. Place the filled and rolled tortillas in the baking dish. They should fill the dish and fit tightly against each other to prevent unrolling.
- Pour the enchilada sauce over the rolled tortillas and top with shredded cheese. Bake in the oven until the edges begin to bubble (about 20 minutes). Serve hot.

Easy White Spinach Pizza

Ingredients
- 1 ball prepared pizza dough (for 12" pizza)
- 1 Tbsp olive oil
- ½ lb. frozen spinach
- ¼ tsp garlic powder
- ¼ tsp salt
- Freshly cracked pepper
- Pinch crushed red pepper
- 1 cup shredded mozzarella
- ⅛ medium red onion (optional)
- 2 oz. Chevre (goat cheese)

Directions
- Preheat the oven to 450 degrees. Thaw the frozen spinach in the microwave or at room temperature until it is no longer in large clumps. Add the garlic powder, salt, and crushed red pepper flakes. Stir to

distribute the spices. Add the mozzarella and stir to combine again.
- Prepare a pizza pan with non-stick spray or cornmeal. Stretch the dough out into a 12" circle and place on the pizza pan. Brush 1 tablespoon of olive oil over the surface. Spread the spinach and cheese mixture over the dough. Thinly slice the red onions and sprinkle over top. Crumble the goat cheese over the pizza.
- Bake the pizza for 10 minutes or until the crust and goat cheese crumbles are lightly browned. Slice into 6 pieces and serve.

Summer Vegetable Tian

Ingredients

- 1 Tbsp olive oil
- 1 medium yellow onion
- 1 tsp minced garlic
- 1 medium zucchini
- 1 medium yellow squash
- 1 medium potato
- 1 medium tomato
- 1 tsp dried thyme
- to taste salt & pepper
- 1 cup shredded Italian cheese

Directions

- Preheat the oven to 400 degrees. Finely dice the onion and mince the garlic. Saute both in a skillet with olive oil until softened (about five minutes).

- While the onion and garlic are sauteing, thinly slice the rest of the vegetables.
- Spray the inside of an 8×8 square or round baking dish with non-stick spray. Spread the softened onion and garlic in the bottom of the dish. Place the thinly sliced vegetables in the baking dish vertically, in an alternating pattern. Sprinkle generously with salt, pepper, and thyme.
- Cover the dish with foil and bake for 30 minutes. Remove the foil, top with cheese and bake for another 15-20 minutes or until the cheese is golden brown.

Roast Chicken with Potatoes and Butternut Squash

Ingredients

- 2 tablespoons minced garlic, divided
- 1 teaspoon salt, divided
- 3/4 teaspoon freshly ground black pepper, divided
- 1/2 teaspoon dried rubbed sage
- 1 (3 1/2-pound) roasting chicken
- Cooking spray
- 12 ounces red potatoes, cut into wedges
- 1 1/2 cups cubed peeled butternut squash (about 8 ounces)
- 2 tablespoons butter, melted

Directions

- Preheat oven to 400°.
- Combine 1 1/2 tablespoons garlic, 1/2 teaspoon salt, 1/2 teaspoon pepper, and sage in a small bowl. Remove and discard giblets and neck from chicken. Starting at neck cavity, loosen skin from breast and drumsticks by inserting fingers, gently pushing between skin and meat. Lift wing tips up and over back; tuck under chicken. Rub garlic mixture under loosened skin. Place chicken, breast side up, on rack of a broiler pan coated with cooking spray. Place rack in broiler pan.

- Combine potatoes, squash, butter, 1 1/2 teaspoons garlic, 1/2 teaspoon salt, and 1/4 teaspoon pepper. Arrange vegetable mixture around chicken.
- Bake at 400° for 1 hour or until a thermometer inserted into meaty part of thigh registers 165°. Let stand 10 minutes. Discard skin.

Cauliflower Bake

Ingredients

- 2 boneless, skinless chicken breasts, cooked & cubed
- 1 package cauliflower
- 8 ounces cheddar cheese, shredded
- 8 ounces Monterey Jack cheese, shredded
- 1 bundle green onions, sliced
- 4 ounces bacon pieces
- 1/8 t garlic power
- Salt & pepper

Directions

- Preheat oven to 350 degrees.
- Steam cauliflower until tender.
- Meanwhile, combine cheeses in a large bowl. Remove ¼ of cheese and set aside. Stir chicken, green onions, bacon, and garlic powder into remaining cheese.
- Stir cauliflower into cheese mixture and season with salt & pepper. Pour into a 9×13 glass baking dish. Top with additional cheese.
- Cover with foil and bake for 25 minutes.
- Remove foil and bake for an additional 5 minutes.

Lightened Up Sesame Chicken

Ingredients

- 1.75 pounds boneless, skinless chicken breasts, cut into pieces
- ¼ tsp salt
- ¼ tsp pepper
- 1 tbsp whole wheat flour
- 1 tbsp sesame oil
- ½ tablespoon olive oil
- 1½ teaspoons minced garlic
- 1 tbsp low-sodium soy sauce
- 1 tbsp brown sugar
- 1 tbsp white vinegar
- ½ cup low-sodium chicken broth
- 2 tbsp sesame seeds

Directions

- Preheat the oven to 400 degrees.
- In a small bowl, whisk chicken broth, brown sugar, sesame oil, garlic, soy sauce, and white vinegar together.
- In another bowl, toss the chicken with salt, pepper, and flour.
- In a large oven-safe pan, heat the olive oil over medium heat.
- Once hot, add the chicken in one layer.
- Cook for three minutes on each side until seared to your liking.
- Turn off the heat and pour the chicken broth mixture over the chicken, stirring to combine.
- Place the entire pan in the oven and cook for 20 minutes.
- Then toss the chicken with sesame seeds and serve with veggies or brown rice.

Grilled Chicken and Two-Bean Salad

Ingredients
- 3/4 pound green beans, trimmed, cut into bite-size pieces
- Salt and pepper
- 1/4 cup extra-virgin olive oil
- 1 tablespoon Dijon mustard
- 1 tablespoon red wine vinegar or sherry vinegar
- 1 small shallot, finely chopped (about 2 1/2 Tbsp.)
- 1 pint cherry tomatoes, halved
- 1 14-oz. can white beans, drained
- 1 pound boneless, skinless chicken breasts

Directions
- Combine green beans and 1 cup lightly salted water in a microwave-safe bowl; cover. Microwave on high until beans are crisp-tender, about 4 minutes. Drain.
- In a bowl, whisk 3 Tbsp. oil along with mustard, vinegar, 1/2 tsp. salt and shallot. Add green beans, tomatoes and white beans and toss to coat.
- Preheat a gas grill to high. Brush chicken with remaining 1 Tbsp. oil; sprinkle with salt and pepper. Grill, covered, until chicken is cooked through, turning once, 8 to 10 minutes total. Let cool slightly; chop.
- Add chicken to bowl and toss again. Serve.

Spinach and Egg Sandwiches

Ingredients

4 plum tomatoes, halved lengthwise

Kosher salt and freshly ground pepper

4 English muffins, split

2 1/2 tablespoons extra-virgin olive oil

1 shallot or 1/4 red onion, thinly sliced

1/4 pound sliced Canadian bacon, cut into thin strips

8 cups baby spinach (about 8 ounces)

4 large eggs

1/3 cup shredded extra-sharp cheddar cheese

Directions

Preheat the broiler. Arrange the tomatoes cut-side up on one half of a rimmed baking sheet and season with salt and pepper. Broil the tomatoes until they begin to soften, about 2 minutes. Remove from the broiler. Arrange the English muffins on the other half of the baking sheet and brush with 1 tablespoon olive oil. Set aside.

Heat 1 tablespoon olive oil in a large nonstick skillet over medium heat. Add the shallot and cook, stirring, until soft, about 2 minutes. Add the Canadian bacon and cook, stirring, until lightly browned, about 3 minutes. Stir in the spinach until wilted; season with salt and pepper. Transfer the mixture to a bowl; keep warm. Wipe out the skillet.

Heat the remaining 1/2 tablespoon olive oil in the skillet over medium-high heat. Crack the eggs into the pan, season with salt and pepper, and fry until the whites are set but the yolks are still runny, about 5 minutes. Remove the pan from the heat.

Top the tomatoes with the cheese. Return the tomatoes and English muffins to the broiler; broil until the cheese is melted, 2 to 3 minutes. Divide the English muffins among plates, then top each with some of the spinach mixture and a fried egg. Serve with the broiled tomatoes.

Farfalle with watercress, cherry tomatoes and feta

Ingredients
- 8 ounces farfalle pasta
- 1 cup crumbled reduced-fat feta cheese
- 2 pints cherry tomatoes, halved
- 3 cups watercress leaves (from 2 small bunches)
- 1/4 teaspoon black pepper

Directions
- Cook pasta according to package directions. Place the cheese in a large bowl; top with the watercress.
- Before draining the pasta, take 1/4 cup of the cooking water from the pot and pour it over the watercress. (Watercress will wilt slightly, and cheese will get soft.) Place the tomatoes in a colander.
- Drain the pasta over the tomatoes for a super-quick blanch. Toss with the watercress and cheese; sprinkle with pepper and serve.

Thai Coconut Shrimp Soup

Ingredients

- 4 cups low-sodium chicken broth
- 1 piece (about 1 inch) peeled ginger, cut into 6 thin slices
- 2 tablespoons fish sauce
- 1 tablespoon light brown sugar
- 1/4 teaspoon Asian chili sauce
- 1 cup instant brown rice
- 1 cup light coconut milk
- 1 cup sliced mushrooms
- 1 red bell pepper, cut into thin slices
- 1 cup sugar snap peas
- 12 ounces large shrimp, peeled and deveined
- 2 tablespoons lime juice
- 1/4 cup chopped scallions

Directions

- In a large pot, bring the chicken broth, ginger, fish sauce, sugar, and chili sauce to a boil. Add the rice and cook 5 minutes.
- Add the coconut milk, mushrooms, pepper slices, and peas; reduce heat and simmer gently for 2 minutes. Add the shrimp and simmer until cooked through, 2 to 3 minutes.
- Remove from heat and stir in the lime juice; ladle into bowls and top with scallions.

Buddha Stir-Fry

Ingredients

- 2 tablespoons cornstarch
- 1 3/4 cup water
- 1/2 cup low-sodium soy sauce
- 1/2 teaspoon Asian chili sauce, or to taste
- 1 tablespoon sesame oil
- 1 tablespoon minced garlic
- 2 tablespoons minced ginger
- 1/2 pound green beans, cut into 2-inch pieces
- 1 red bell pepper, thinly sliced
- 2 14-ounce packages firm tofu, drained and cut into 1/2-inch cubes
- 1 cup shredded carrots
- 1 cup snow peas

Directions

- Dissolve the cornstarch in 2 tablespoons of the water. Stir in the remaining water, soy sauce, and chili sauce; set aside. Heat the oil in a large nonstick skillet over medium-high heat.
- Add the garlic and ginger; cook, stirring, 15 seconds. Add the green beans and red pepper and stir-fry 2 minutes; push them to the perimeter of the skillet.
- Add the tofu and cook, stirring once or twice, 4 to 5 minutes, or until lightly browned.

- Stir the sauce and pour it into the skillet. Cook, stirring occasionally, 2 to 3 minutes.
- Add the carrots and snow peas; cook 1 to 2 minutes, or until the vegetables are crisp-tender

Ham & Swiss Sliders

Ingredients
- 1 T. dried minced onions
- 2 tsp. prepared mustard
- a splash or two of Worcestershire sauce
- 1/2 T. poppy seeds
- 1/4 C butter, melted
- 1 dozen dinner rolls or 2 dozen party rolls- Mayo
- ham
- sliced Swiss cheese

Directions
- Preheat oven to 350°. In a small mixing bowl mix onion, mustard, Worcestershire, poppy seeds, and melted butter.
- Leaving the dinner rolls intact, slice them open so that you have one solid top and bottom. Place the bottom half on a baking sheet.

- Spread rolls (top and bottom) with mayo. Line the bottom half of the rolls with ham and cheese. Return the top part of the rolls and brush the butter mixture evenly over top.
- Cover with foil and bake for 15-20 minutes or till warmed through.
- Separate with a sharp knife and serve.

Shepherd's Pie Recipe

Ingredients

- 1 1/2 lbs ground round beef
- 1 onion chopped
- 1 cup peas *we prefer fresh diced green beans (1/4 inch) instead
- 1 cup diced carrots
- 1 can corn
- 1 1/2 – 2 lbs potatoes (4 big ones)
- 8 tablespoons butter (1 stick)
- 1/2 cup beef broth
- 1 teaspoon Worcestershire sauce
- Salt and pepper to taste

Directions

- Peel and quarter potatoes, boil in salted water until tender (about 20 minutes)

- While the potatoes are cooking, melt 4 Tablespoons butter (1/2 a stick) in large frying pan
- Sauté onions in butter until tender over medium heat (10 mins). If you are adding vegetables, add them according to cooking time. Put any carrots and/or green beans in with the onions. Add corn either at the end of the cooking of the onions, or after the meat has initially cooked.
- Add ground beef and sauté until no longer pink. Add salt, pepper and Worcestershire sauce. Then add half a cup of beef broth and cook, uncovered, over low heat for 10 minutes, adding more beef broth as necessary to keep moist
- Mash potatoes in bowl with rest of butter, season to taste (you can add sour cream or cheese to the potatoes if you'd like)
- Place beef mixture into baking dish. Distribute mashed potatoes on top. Rough up with a fork so that there are peaks that will brown nicely. You can use the fork to make some designs in the potatoes as well.
- Cook in 400 degree oven until bubbling and brown (about 30 minutes). Broil for last few minutes if necessary to brown.

Sweet & Spicy Chicken Wings

Ingredients
- 12 chicken wings or 24 chicken drumettes
- 1 cup Pace® Picante Sauce
- 1/4 cup honey
- 1/2 tsp. ground ginger

Directions
- Cut off chicken wing tips and discard. Cut chicken wings in half at joint. Place chicken into foil-lined shallow baking pan.
- Stir picante sauce, honey and ginger in large bowl. Toss chicken with 1/3 cup of picante mixture.
- Bake at 500°F. on lowest oven rack 35 min. or until crispy and cooked through, turning chicken over once halfway through baking. Remove chicken and toss with remaining picante mixture.

Baked apples stuffed with dried fruit and pecans

Ingredients

- 8 red apples (gala or rome beauty)
- 2 tablespoons fresh lemon juice
- ½ cup finely chopped dried apricots
- 4 tablespoons chopped pecans, toasted
- 4 tablespoons packed dark brown sugar
- 1/2 teaspoon cinnamon
- 1/2 teaspoon ground nutmeg
- 2 tablespoons softened unsalted butter
- 4 tablespoons unsalted butter cut into 2 pieces
- 1 cup apple cider

Preparation

- Preheat oven to 350°F.
- Core apples. Peel about 1/3 down the apple. Stand apples up in a large ceramic or glass pie plate and make 4 evenly spaced vertical cuts starting from top of each apple and stopping halfway from bottom to keep apple intact. Brush inside and outside of peeled apple with lemon juice.
- Toss together apricots, pecans, brown sugar, cinnamon, and nutmeg in a bowl. Rub softened butter into dried fruit mixture with your fingers until combined well. Pack center of each apple with mixture. Put a piece of remaining butter on top of each apple. Pour cider around apples and cover pie plate tightly with foil.
- Bake in middle of oven, basting once, until apples are just tender when pierced with a fork, about 45 minutes. Remove foil and continue to bake until apples are very tender but not falling apart, 20-30 minutes more.
- Transfer to serving dishes and spoon sauce over and around apples.

Spinach and Potato Breakfast Hash

Ingredients
- 1 green bell pepper, diced into medium chunks
- 1 medium yellow onion, diced into medium chunks
- 3 cloves garlic, minced
- 1 1/2 pounds fingerling potatoes (russet or new potatoes will also be great), cut into bite-size chunks
- 4 tablespoons olive oil, divided
- 6 ounces sausage, cooked and sliced (I used vegetarian chipotle sausage) (pork or chicken sausage would also be great)
- 1 heaping teaspoon fennel seeds
- salt and pepper to taste
- 2 cups baby spinach leaves
- 2 to 4 eggs, fried to desired doneness

Directions
- Place a rack in the center of the oven and preheat to 400 degrees F. Place diced potatoes on a lined baking sheet and drizzle with about 2 tablespoons of olive oil, salt, and pepper. Bake potatoes for 20-30 minutes, or until potatoes are cooked through. Poke the potato chunks with a fork, if they're tender they're done.
- While potatoes are baking, heat about 2 tablespoons of olive oil in a large saucepan, over medium heat. (Wait! Now would be a great time to cook your sausage if it's raw. Cook through and remove from the pan, then follow the next steps). Add the diced peppers and onions and cook until browned and broken down, about 6 minutes. Season with salt and pepper as it cooks. Add the minced garlic, and cook for 1 minute more. Remove from pan and place in a bowl to the side.
- When potatoes are done roasting, remove from the oven.
- Return the pan you cooked the onions and peppers in to a medium flame. Add the sliced, cooked sausage and potatoes. Pan fry until the sausage and potatoes have crispy bits on them. Add the fennel seeds. Stir. Add the onion and pepper mixture and fold to incorporate. Remove from the flame and add spinach leaves. Toss to incorporate and wilt the leaves.

- Transfer the hash to a serving dish. Season with salt and pepper as necessary. Fry as many eggs and you'd like and serve over hash.
- This has will last for up to 4 days in the fridge. It's also really delicious mixed with black beans and salsa for dinner. With tortillas and cheese... amazing.

Roasted Cauliflower and Aged White Cheddar Soup

Ingredients
- 1 small head cauliflower, cut into florets
- 2 tablespoons oil
- salt and pepper to taste
- 1 tablespoon oil
- 1 medium onion, diced
- 2 cloves garlic, chopped
- 1 teaspoon thyme, chopped
- 3 cups vegetable broth or chicken broth or chicken stock *
- 1 1/2 cups aged white cheddar, shredded
- 1 cup milk or cream
- salt and pepper to taste

Directions

- Toss the cauliflower florets in the oil along with the salt and pepper, arrange them in a single layer on a large baking sheet and roast in a preheated 400F oven until lightly golden brown, about 20-30 minutes.

Heat the oil in a large sauce pan over medium heat, add the onion and saute until tender, about 5-7 minutes.

Add the garlic and thyme and saute until fragrant, about a minute.

Add the broth, deglaze the pan, add the cauliflower, bring to a boil, reduce the heat and simmer, covered, for 20 minutes.

Puree the soup until it reaches your desired consistency with a stick blender.

Mix in the cheese, let it melt without bringing it to boil again.

- Mix in the milk, season with salt and pepper and remove from heat.

Creamy Slow Cooker Tortellini Soup

Ingredients

- 1-1 1/2 - 2 ounce envelope white sauce mix
- 4 cups water
- 1-14 ounce can vegetable broth
- 1 1/2 cups sliced fresh mushrooms
- 1/2 cup chopped onion
- 3 cloves garlic, minced
- 1/2 teaspoon dried basil, crushed
- 1/4 teaspoon salt
- 1/4 teaspoon dried oregano, crushed
- 1/8 teaspoon cayenne pepper
- 1- 7 or 8 ounce package dried cheese tortellini (about 2 cups)
- 1-12 ounce can evaporated milk

- 6 cups fresh baby spinach leaves or torn spinach
- Ground black pepper (optional)
- Finely shredded Parmesan cheese (optional)

Directions

- Place dry white sauce mix in a 3-1/2- or 4-quart slow cooker. Gradually add the water to the white sauce mix, stirring until smooth. Stir in broth, mushrooms, onion, garlic, basil, salt, oregano, and cayenne pepper.
- Cover and cook on low-heat setting for 5 to 6 hours or on high-heat setting for 2-1/2 to 3 hours.
- Stir in dried tortellini. Cover and cook on low-heat setting for 1 hour more or high-heat setting for 45 minutes more.
- Stir in evaporated milk and fresh spinach. If desired, sprinkle individual servings with black pepper and Parmesan cheese. Makes 4 servings.

Poor Man Husband Casserole

Ingredients

- 1 pound ground beef
- garlic to taste
- 1 teaspoon salt
- 1 teaspoon sugar
- 2 cans (8-ounces) tomato sauce
- 8 ounces egg noodles
- 8 ounces sour cream
- 8 ounces cream cheese
- 1 1/2 cup Cheddar cheese, shredded

Instructions

- Preheat oven to 350 degrees F.
- Cook and drain ground beef.
- Mix beef with garlic, salt, sugar and tomato sauce. Cover and simmer for 15 minutes.
- Cook and drain egg noodles.
- Mix sour cream and cream cheese together in a small bowl.
- Layer, in order twice - noodles, sour cream mixture, meat. Sprinkle Cheddar cheese on top.
- Bake at 350 degrees for 20 minutes.

Cabbage Noodle Salad

Ingredients

Ingredients for dressing:
- 3 tablespoons olive oil
- 3 tablespoon vinegar
- 2 tablespoon sugar
- 1/2 ramen noodle seasoning package
- 1/4 teaspoon pepper
- 1 tablespoon low sodium soy sauce

Ingredients for salad:
- 1 small head red or green cabbage (or 1/2 of each)
- 2 green onions, chopped
- 1 carrot, peeled and grated
- 1 package ramen noodles, crushed

Directions

- Make dressing by combining ingredients in a large bowl. Stir to dissolve sugar.
- Combine the first three salad ingredients, toss well. Add crushed ramen noodles and dressing to salad and toss again.

Serve right away or cover and refrigerate to allow the flavors to blend.

Basque Pil Pil Cod

4 fresh or dried salted Cod fillets

10 ounces of extra virgin olive oil

5 garlic cloves peeled

1 chili pepper, deseeded and cut in four pieces

If using dried salted Cod soak the Cod for 24 hours changing the water at least 3 times.

Add the oil to a wide frying pan, brown the garlic cloves and chili pepper on medium heat, remove from oil and reserve.

Slice the Cod into one inch wide pieces, add to oil in frying pan with skin side down and cook on medium heat for 5 minutes on each side, repeat until all fish is cooked.

Serve on plates and drizzle oil from pan on top of fish and add the reserves garlic and chili pepper if desired.

Serves 4

Broiled Cajun Swordfish

4 Thick swordfish steaks

1 teaspoon of salt

1 teaspoon of paprika

1/4 teaspoon of oregano

1/2 teaspoon of dried thyme

1/2 teaspoon of garlic powder

1/2 teaspoon of black pepper

The juice of two lemons

Place the lemon juice in a bowl. In a separate bowl, combine all of the spices. Dip the steaks into the lemon juice then coat them with the spices. Arrange the seasoned fish on a broiler pan and broil 4-inches from the heat until it flakes easily with a fork, approximately 5 minutes. Turn once during broiling.

Serves 4

Catfish Creole

4 catfish filets

4 chopped tomatoes

4 tablespoons of olive oil

1 chopped onion

1 chopped bell pepper

1 Jalapeno

Salt and pepper to taste

Fry the jalapeno, bell pepper and onion in 2 tablespoons of olive oil in a skillet for 5 minutes until soft. Add the tomatoes and simmer for an additional 10 minutes. In another skillet, cook the catfish in the remaining olive oil for 10 to 15 minutes. Serve the catfish with the tomatoes.

Serves 4

Coconut Shrimp Patties

1 pound of peeled and deveined raw shrimp

1/2 teaspoon salt

1 cup shredded coconut

2 egg whites

2 tablespoons olive oil

Remove the shrimp tails and place them into a food processor. Pulse the shrimp until they are in tiny pieces. Whisk the egg whites. Add the salt, coconut and shrimp to the eggs, stir well. Form the mixture into eight 1/2-inch thick patties. Heat half of the oil in a large frying pan and fry 4 of the patties for 5 minutes per side. Heat the remaining oil and fry the remaining patties.

Serves 8 patties

Guacamole Tuna Wraps

4 cans of tuna in water

2 diced jalapeños

2 thinly sliced scallions

2 avocados

2 limes

Salt & pepper to taste

4 large lettuce leaves

Place drained tuna in a bowl, separate with a fork and add the scallions and jalapeno. Add the juice of one lime and salt and pepper to taste. In a separate bowl, combine the juice form the reaming lime, salt, pepper and avocado. Mash with a fork to make guacamole. Combine the tuna and the guacamole. Mix well and scoop onto the lettuce leaves to serve.

Serves 4 wraps

Halibut Roll-Ups

4 Thin Halibut fillets

1 zucchini

1 red pepper

4 teaspoons spicy red pepper pesto

The juice of two lemons

Dijon mustard

Toothpicks

Salt and pepper to taste

Cut the pepper into strips that are one inch thick. Steam or microwave for 5 minutes. Once cooking is completed, cool in cold water and peel the skin from the flesh. Remove any skin from the fish. Cut the fish in half, lengthwise and spread a teaspoon Dijon mustard on one side of each piece. Follow with a strip of the pepper and a thin strip of zucchini. Roll them up, beginning at the tail. Use two or three toothpicks to hold it together. Place the fish on a baking sheet and place in the oven for 25 to 30 minutes, depending on the thickness of the fillets. Add salt and pepper to taste

Serves 4

Hawaiian Salmon Ceviche

2 pounds of fresh salmon fillets

1 pound of chopped tomatoes

1 cup lemon juice

2 green onions

Place the salmon in a large bowl and add the lemon juice. Cover. Marinate for at least 2 hours.

Drain the salmon and soak in cold water for 2 hours. Change the water two or three times. Drain salmon and pull the meat away from the skin and bones. Mash the salmon with your hands. Add green onions and tomatoes. Continue to mix with hands until smooth. Chill for a few minutes, and then serve.

Serves 4

Honey Garlic Shrimp

2 pounds of peeled and deveined shrimp

2 tablespoons honey

2 tablespoons minced garlic

2 tablespoons coconut oil

Melt the coconut oil in a frying pan. Add the garlic and cook on medium heat for 1 minute. Add the shrimp and cook for 5 minutes, then add the honey and cook for another 5 minutes stirring occasionally.

Serves 4

Horseradish Salmon Patties

2 pounds of canned salmon, drained

1/2 cup Paleo mayo

1 tablespoon prepared horseradish

4 eggs, slightly beaten

1 cup almond flour

1 finely chopped onion

Olive oil

Combine all of the ingredients except of the olive oil in a bowl. With your hands roll the mixture into four balls and flatten into four-inch patties. Fry in 2 tablespoons of olive oil for 6 to 8 minutes, turning once during cooking.

Serves 4

Jalapeno Snapper

4 snapper fillets

2 Jalapenos

2 ripe avocados

1 lemon

Garlic powder to taste

Salt and pepper to taste

Sprinkle the snapper fillets with garlic, salt and pepper.

Fry the snapper fillets for 2 to 3 minutes per side

Combine the jalapenos, juice form lemon and avocado in a food processor. Puree until smooth. And serve on top of fillets.

Serves 4

Lemon Blackened Bass

4 striped bass

2 teaspoons of Blackened seasoning

4 sticks of Lemon grass

1 cup of olive oil

Place the bass on a platter and sprinkle with the blackened seasoning. Add a lemon grass stick to each bass. Cook for 15 minutes in an oven that has been preheated to 425 degrees F. Turn the fish once and cook for an additional 10 minutes.

Serves 4

Lobster Salad

4 steamed Lobster Tails, cleaned and shells removed

2 Celery stalks

1 onion

1 sweet pepper

2 tomatoes

1/2 cup of lemon juice

Extra virgin olive oil

Salt and pepper to taste

Chop the tomato, sweet pepper, celery, onion and lobster into small pieces. Combine them together and mix until well blended. Drizzle with olive oil and serve.

Serves 4

Mackerel Dip

4 smoked mackerel fillets

Worcestershire sauce to taste (Optional)

3 tablespoons of sour cream

The juice of one lemon

1 teaspoon of Dijon mustard

Remove the mackerel from the skin and break into bite sized pieces. Mix in the mustard, Worcestershire sauce, lemon juice and sour cream. Blend until it forms a paste. Refrigerate until set.

Serves 4

Marinera Soup

1 pound of halibut

1 pound of bluefish

1 pound of tomatoes, peeled and chopped

4 Tablespoons olive oil

1 chopped onion

2 chopped carrots

2 chopped celery stalks

3 chopped garlic cloves

2 finely chopped flat anchovy fillets

4 cups of clam juice

4 cups of water

Salt and pepper to taste

Cut the fish into 2x2-inch pieces. In a pot large enough to hold all of the ingredients, heat the oil. Add the onion and cook for 3 minutes. Add the garlic, celery and carrots and cook until onions begin to turn golden brown, approximately 5 minutes. Add the tomatoes, water, clam juice and anchovies. Bring to a boil, reduce heat and simmer uncovered for 10 minutes. Add fish and cover pan. Simmer 15 minutes. Add salt and pepper to taste.

Serves 4

Olive Relish Tuna

2 pounds of tuna steak, cut into 4 portions

2 tablespoons of olive oil

Salt and pepper to taste

Olive Relish

1 finely chopped celery stalk

1 finely chopped garlic clove

1/2 cup finely chopped fresh parsley

1/2 cup chopped pitted black olives

1/2 teaspoon dried oregano

The juice from one lemon

1 tablespoon extra virgin olive oil

Salt and pepper to taste

To prepare olive relish: Combine the salt, pepper, oil, lemon juice, oregano, garlic, celery, olives and parsley in a small bowl.

To grill tuna: Preheat the grill to medium. Rub tuna with oil and season with salt and pepper. Grill until seared on both sides and cooked through, approximately 4 minutes per side. Serve with olive relish.

Serves 4

Orange Grilled Swordfish

4 Thick swordfish steaks

4 tablespoon of olive oil

1/2 finely chopped red onion

1/2 teaspoon of crushed red pepper

3 Peeled navel oranges,

12 pitted and coarsely chopped oil-cured black olives

Salt and pepper to taste

1/2 cup of chopped fresh mint leaves

The juice from half a lemon

Remove the orange sections, without the membranes with a sharp knife and put in a bowl, add the lemon juice, 2 tablespoons of oil, crushed peppers, onions, mint and olives and stir. Place bowl in the refrigerator.

Preheat grill to high. Brush the swordfish with half of the remaining oil and the grill with the other half. Sprinkle salt and pepper on the fish. Grill the fish for two to three minutes per side until just cooked. Top with the orange mix and serve.

Serves 4

Pork Salmon Cakes

2 pound of canned salmon, drained

2 beaten eggs

1 cup of finely crushed pork skins

Olive oil

1 thinly chopped onion

Dill, salt and pepper to taste

Combine all of the ingredients in a bowl, with your hands roll the mixture into four balls and flatten into four-inch patties. Fry in 2 tablespoons of olive oil for 8 minutes, turning once during cooking.

Serves 4

Prosciutto Scallops

2 pounds of scallops

1/2 pound of sliced prosciutto

1 trimmed bouquet of asparagus

Salt and pepper to taste

Olive Oil

Preheat oven to 350 degrees F. clean, de-foot and dry the scallops. Cover a baking sheet with aluminum foil. Wrap each scallop with the prosciutto. Lay each wrapped scallop on the baking tray. Baste the tops with oil and season to taste with salt and pepper. Bake for 15 minutes until the scallops are hot inside. In a skillet, sear the asparagus in olive oil for about 5 minutes. Serve.

Serves 4

Red Snapper Mango Ceviche

2 pounds of skinless snapper fillets

3 minced garlic cloves

1 tablespoon minced ginger

1 minced fresh chili pepper

1 cup lemon juice

2 mangoes, peeled, seeded, and shredded

1 thinly sliced red bell pepper

1 thinly sliced red onion

1/2 cup chopped fresh cilantro

1 cup fresh orange juice

Salt and pepper to taste

Place snapper fillets in a single layer in a baking pan. Combine the lemon juice, chilies, ginger and garlic in a small bowl. Pour over the snapper making sure the juice fully covers each slice. Cover and place the pan in the refrigerator for at least 2 hours.

Remove the snapper from the pan and slice into pieces. Discard the liquid. Combine the rest of the ingredients in a large bowl and toss together. Place on plates and top with the snapper.

Serves 4

Rosemary Baked Salmon

4 salmon filets

1/2 cup of olive oil

2 tablespoon of fresh rosemary

2 teaspoons of salt

Begin by preheating the oven to 350 degrees F. Combine the salt, rosemary and olive oil. Rub the mixture on the salmon fillets. Wrap each fillet in a piece of foil and bake for 25 to 30 minutes.

Serves 4

Stewed Cod & Capers

4 fresh or dried salted Cod fillets

4 sliced green onions

2 tablespoon of olive oil

1 thinly sliced red onion

2 tablespoon of capers, drained

1 thinly sliced carrot

2 lemons

If using dried salted Cod soak the Cod for 24 hours changing the water at least 3 times.

In a deep skillet, heat the oil and sauté the onions for 3 minutes. Add the capers and cook for an additional minute. Next, add the carrots and sauté for two more minutes. Mix in the green onions and spread the vegetables over the bottom of the skillet. Place the Cod on the vegetables. Add a small amount of water to cover the bottom of the pan. Cover and cook for 10 minutes, until fish is opaque. Transfer the fish to a plate for serving, add the vegetables and top everything with lemon juice.

Serves 4

Thai Tuna Ceviche

2 pounds of sushi like tuna

1 cup fresh lime juice

1 thinly sliced red onion,

1 diced tomato

1 tablespoon minced ginger

1 cup coconut of milk

1/2 cup chopped fresh cilantro

Salt and pepper to taste

Slice the tuna thin and lay in a single layer in a shallow pan. Pour lime juice over the top, making sure the juice fully covers each slice. Cover the pan and allow the tuna to soak for two hours. Occasionally move the tuna pieces around and turn them to ensure that all of the tuna soaks in the lime juice. After two hours, remove the tuna and discard the lime juice. Combine the tuna with remaining ingredients in a bowl. Mix well before serving.

Serves 4

Tomato Halibut Stew

2 pound of Halibut, cubed

2 tablespoons of olive oil

4 chopped garlic cloves

1 sliced onion

4 sliced tomatoes

4 diced carrots

4 diced celery stalks

4 cups of tomato juice

Salt and pepper to taste

Heat oil and cook the garlic and onions until soft, about 5 minutes. Add the tomato juice, tomatoes, carrots and celery and bring to a boil. Reduce heat and simmer for 5 minutes. Add the fish and cook until the fish is opaque, approximately 30 minutes, and season with salt, pepper before serving.

Serves 4

Tomato Sauce Salmon

2 pounds of canned salmon

1 pound of tomato sauce

1 teaspoon of dill

4 chopped garlic cloves

1 sliced bell pepper

1 sliced onion

2 teaspoons of paprika

1 bay leaf

2 tablespoons of olive oil

Salt & pepper to taste

Heat the oil in a skillet. Add the pepper and onion and cook until soft, about 5 minutes. Drain the salmon and add it to the pan. Break it up with a spoon. Then add the tomato sauce and paprika. Add a bay leaf and salt and pepper to taste. Cover. Simmer for 10 minutes.

Serves 4

Tuna Artichokes

2 pounds of fresh tuna, cubed

18 ounces of canned artichoke hearts, drained and halved

4 tablespoons olive oil

1 thinly sliced red onion

The juice on one lemon

4 thinly sliced garlic cloves

Salt and pepper to taste

Heat half of the olive oil in a skillet. Add the onion and garlic and sauté until soft, about 5 minutes. Add the lemon and artichoke hearts and cook until heated thoroughly, about 3 minutes. Place on a plate. Season the tuna with salt and pepper. Add the remaining oil to the skillet and cook the tuna until it is brown on all sides. Put the artichoke mix back into the frying pan and toss together.

Serves 4

Tuna Burgers

1pound drained canned tuna

1finely chopped celery stalk

1 teaspoon of dill

The juice from one lemon

1 finely chopped onion

1/2 finely chopped red pepper

2 lightly beaten eggs

2 Tablespoons of olive oil

Salt and pepper to taste

Add all ingredients to a bowl and mix well. Divide mix into four equal sections and form patties out of each section. Heat oil in a frying pan or heat the barbecue grill until hot. Cook patties for 10 minutes, turning once during cooking time.

Serves 4

Tuna Sardine Patties

2 cans of tuna in water, drained

2 cans of sardines

1 onion

4 cups of kale

1/2 cup of cilantro

2 eggs

Salt & pepper to taste

Place all of the ingredients in a food processor and blend. Form mixture into balls and flatten. Place on a baking sheet and bake for 10 to 15 minutes in a 400 degree F oven. Add lemon juice before serving.

Serves 4

Tunisian Cod

2 pounds of fresh or dried salted Cod fillets

4 thinly sliced garlic cloves

1/2 teaspoon ground caraway seeds

1/2 teaspoon ground cumin seeds

1/2 teaspoon ground coriander seeds

1/2 top dried hot pepper flakes

2 thinly sliced onions

2 thinly sliced tomatoes

1 cup fish stock

Salt and pepper to taste

If using dried salted Cod soak the Cod for 24 hours changing the water at least 3 times.

Add ground spices, salt and pepper to fish filets. Lightly spray a baking dish with non-stick cooking spray. Add half of the garlic, the tomatoes and the onions and lay the fish on top. Add remaining onions and garlic. Add the fish stock over the top of the fish. Bake in a preheated 400 degree F oven for 30 minutes until fish is done.

Serves 4

Tuscan Cod

2 pounds fresh dried salted Cod

1 thinly sliced red onion,

2 tablespoon extra virgin olive oil

4 finely minced garlic cloves

1 red bell pepper, roasted over a flame, peeled, seeded and cut into thin strips

4 teaspoons capers, drained and lightly rinsed

12 pitted and coarsely chopped oil-cured ripe olives

Parsley sprigs and lemon wedges for garnish

If using dried salted Cod soak the Cod for 24 hours changing the water at least 3 times.

Heat the oil in a skillet and add the onion and garlic. Sauté for 2 to 3 minutes, then add the olives, capers and bell peppers. Cook for an additional 2 to 3 minutes and then spread the vegetables evenly on the bottom of the pan. Cut the fish into four equal sized portions. Place the fish on top of the vegetables and add 1/8-inch of water to the pan. Cover. Steam for 10 minutes until the fish is tender, flakey and all of the water has evaporated. Transfer to a serving dish, top with vegetables and garnish with lemon and parsley.

Serves 4

Wasabi Avocado Crab Cakes

1 pound of lump Crabmeat drained

1/2 Teaspoon onion powder

2 Green Onions finely sliced

Dash of Red Pepper

2 Tablespoons of Blanched Almond Flour

2 Tablespoons of Unsweetened Shredded Coconut,

1/2 finely diced Bell Pepper

2 Egg Yolks

1/2 Teaspoon garlic powder

1/4 Cup of Paleo mayo

1/4 Teaspoon of Salt

1/4 Teaspoon of Black Pepper

2 Tablespoons of Coconut Oil

Sauce

1 Avocado

1/3 Cup Water

1 Tablespoon Paleo mayo

2 Teaspoons Wasabi Paste

1 Tablespoon of Soy Sauce

1 Tablespoon Rice Vinegar

Dash of Salt

In a bowl combine the salt, pepper, red pepper, onion powder, garlic powder, mayonnaise, egg yolk, onion, bell peppers and crab meat. With your hands, form the mixture into small patties. Place the patties on a plate and put them in the refrigerator for 15 minutes. In another bowl, combine the coconut and almond flour. Heat the coconut oil. While the oil warms, press each patty into the almond flour and shake off any excess.

Fry each patty in the coconut oil for 4-5 minutes each side until crispy and golden brown. Combine the sauce ingredients in a blender and blend until smooth. Serve the crab cakes with the desired amount of sauce.

Serves 4

20 Minute Hamburger Skillet Stew

Ingredients

- 1/4 lb Lean ground beef
- large Onion, sliced wafer-thin
- 4   Carrots, sliced wafer-thin
- Potatoes, halved, sliced wafer-thin
- Ribs celery, sliced wafer-thin
- 1 c Boiling water
- 2 t Beef extract OR bouillon
- 2   Bay leaves
- 1/4 t Dried thyme
- Salt OR garlic salt
- Pepper
- 1/4 c Dry red wine OR tomato juice
- 2 T All purpose flour

Directions

- Use <u>melon baller</u> and shape meat into tiny meatballs.
- Brown in skillet. Discard any fat. Stir onion into skillet and cook 1 min.
- Add boiling water or broth and extract or bouillon.
- Add remaining veggies, seasonings. Cover, cook over low heat, 15 minutes until vegetables are tender.

- Combine wine or water and flour in covered jar. Shake and stir into skillet. Cook and stir until sauce is thick, 4 minutes

Antiguan Charcoal Baked Bananas

Ingredients

- large ripe bananas, in a bunch
- 4 tbsp butter
- 1/2 cup brown sugar
- 1/2 tsp ground allspice or 1/2 tsp fresh grated nutmeg
- 3 limes, halved
- 1/4 cup dark rum, heated in a small pan onside of grill

Directions

- Set the bunch of unpeeled bananas in hot coals.
- Bake until black and soft to the touch.
- Meanwhile, heat butter with brown sugar and spices until bubbly. Each person should slit his banana, squeeze a lime half over it and drizzle the butter-sugar mixture on top.
- Ignite rum and pour it flaming over the bananas a little at a time, shaking the skillet gently until the flame dies.

Aunt Sarah's Chili Sauce

Ingredients
- 4 qt Tomatoes, cut in quarters
- 1 T Mustard seed
- 2 c Onions, sliced
- 1 T Celery seed
- 2 c Green peppers, sliced
- 2 1/2 c Cider vinegar
- 1 T Salt
- 1 c Sugar- brown, white, maple,
- 3 T Mixed pickling spices
- Honey, whatever is handy

Directions
- Mix everything together in a big pot and put on the back of woodstove so that everything simmers gently for days. It is ready when it reaches the thickness you want.

Australian Grilled Fish

Ingredients

- 4 Fish steaks
- 1/4 c Lime juice
- 2 T Vegetable oil
- 1 t Dijon mustard
- 2 t Fresh ginger root --,Grated
- 1/4 t Cayenne pepper
- Black pepper

Directions

- In a bowl, combine the lime juice, 1 tablespoon oil, ginger, cayenne pepper and enough freshly ground black pepper to suit your taste.
- Marinate the fish in the marinade for 45-60 minutes. Turn steaks 2-3 times.
- Have the grill prepared with white coals and brush the cooking grill with the remaining one tablespoon oil.
- Grill the fish, brushing several times with the marinade, until cooked through and opaque in the center. Turn fish after about 4-5 minutes. Total grilling time will depend on your grill and the heat of the coals.

* To broil instead, use a broiler pan brushed with oil and broil until center is opaque. It will take about 10 minutes total in broiler. Turn steaks after 5 minutes, and baste often with marinade.

Baked Stuffed Fish

Ingredients
- White fish, enough for -4-6
- 2 c Soft bread cubes, about ½ " cubes
- Small onion, chopped -fine
- Green pepper, blanched and, Chopped
- 8 oz Imitation crabmeat
- 1/4 c Lemon juice
- 1/2 c HELLMANS mayo
- Salt & pepper, to Taste

Directions
- Mix all these ingredients together and roll up in fish fillets, securing them with toothpicks.
- Divide it among four or five good-sized pieces.
- Bake at 400 for 30 minutes. During last 10 minutes
- pour newburg sauce over fish.
- It's good with flounder, but any white fish will do.

Best Peach Cobbler

Ingredients

Filling
- 3 T Sugar
- 2 qt canned peach slices,
- 4 t Baking powder
- 3/4 c Sugar
- T Lard (or butter)
- 1/4 c Water
- 3/4 c milk cut half-, Canned
- 3 t Corn starch
- strength with water (just topping enough to moisten dough)
- 2 c Flour

Directions

- FILLING: Dissolve corn starch in water; add mixture to peaches and juice in a large, warm Dutch oven; stir well; sprinkle sugar on top; cover and allow to simmer lightly while topping is prepared.
- TOPPING: On a floured board, turn out a soft dough; pat down to 1/2" thick; cut into strips 1/2" wide and place cris-cross atop peach mixture;
- cover and cook approximately 20 minutes until golden brown.
- Serve with Campfire Coffee. Serves approximately 18.

Biscuit And Pancake Mix

Ingredients
- 9 c Flour, sifted
- 4 t Salt
- 1/3 c Baking powder
- 1 3/4 c Shortening, vegetable
- 1 c Milk, powdered

Directions
- Chill shortening. Sift all dry ingredients. Cut shortening into flour till mixture resembles coarse cornmeal.
- Store, well covered, in a cool, dry place.
- Use for pancakes, biscuits, shortcake, cobblers or anything that you would make from a packaged biscuit mix. All you need is water.
- For pancakes add 1 tablespoon each sugar and powdered eggs to each cup of mix.

Blackened Fish

Ingredients

- 2 T Paprika
- 2 T Cayenne pepper
- 2 T White pepper
- 3/4 c Creole seasoning
- 1/4 c Blackening seasoning
- 4   .to 12 fish fillets
- 1/8 c Butter (or margarine)

Directions

- Mix the spices. Coat the fillets with the spice mixture.
- Melt the butter or margarine in an iron skillet over a hot cooking fire.
- Sear the fish for 1 to 2 minutes on each side, or until they smoke and appear "blackened".
- Remove the skillet from the fire and cover. The heat in the pan will complete the cooking in about 10 minutes. The spices can be mixed at home and stored in an airtight container.

Blazing Trail Mix

Ingredients

- 2 c miniature wheat or, Shredded bran squares
- 1 c thin pretzel, Unsalted sticks, broken into pieces
- 1/2 c lentils, Cooked
- 1/2 c Quick-cooking rolled oats
- 1/2 c Raisins
- 1/2 c dried apples, Chopped
- 1/4 c Honey
- 2 t Curry powder
- 1/2 t coriander, Ground
- 1/4 t cumin, Ground
- 1/4 t Paprika
- 1/8 t red pepper, Ground

Directions

- In a <u>13x9-inch baking pan</u>, combine the wheat or bran squares, pretzels, lentils, oats, raisins, and apples. In a small bowl, stir together the honey, curry powder, coriander, cumin, paprika and pepper.
- Drizzle the honey mixture over the cereal mixture.
- Toss until evenly coated. Bake at 350 for 15 to 20 minutes or until crisp, stirring occasionally. Store in an airtight container o r self-closing plastic bags.

Box Oven

Ingredients

- Brick (or flat rock)
- 1 pk Aluminum foil, heavy-duty
- Corrugated cardboard box
- Metal pie pan, old
- Coat hangers
- Charcoal briquets, lit

Directions

- Cover the inside and outside of the box completely with 3 or 4 layers of aluminum foil, including the flaps.
- Lay box on level ground so that the opening opens oven-style.
- Straighten the coat hangers, then run them through the sides of the box about 2/3 of the way up from the bottom to form a rack.
- Set brick in bottom. Place live coals into pie pan/pie plate. Put pan on brick.
- Place food to be cooked onto coat-hanger rack and close oven door.
- Watch carefully, checking often. Each live coal makes about 80 degrees Fahrenheit.

Buckwheat Pecan Pancakes For Camping

Ingredients

MIX IN A ZIPLOCK BAG
- 2 c Buckwheat flour
- 1/2 t Salt
- 2/3 c Wheat flour
- 2 t Baking powder
- 2/3 c dry milk, Instant
- 3 T egg (optional), Dried

IN SMALL TIGHT CONTAINER
- 2 T Oil
- 2 T Molasses

ADD WHEN MIXING
- 2 1/2 c Water
- 1/2 c Pecan halves

PACK FOR TOPPING WHEN DONE
- 1/4 c Butter (optional)
- 1 c Maple syrup

Directions

- Assume moderate heat on a campfire or pack stove.
- When ready to cook, mix all ingredients except the butter and syrup and let set a couple minutes. If stiff, add a little more water.
- If you heat the pan well first, no oil is necessary; however you will need a good, flat metal spatula.

- Serve hot with butter and syrup. Can be saved for later in the day; great with jam.

Burgers In Foil

Ingredients

- 1 ½ lb beef, Ground
- small green bell peppers, chopped
- 16-inch squares aluminum
- onion flakes, Dehydrated
- foil
- Worcestershire sauce
- Carrots, sliced
- Salt & pepper, to Taste
- 1 cn Potatoes,16oz, sliced

Directions

- Separate meat into 4 portions. Place each in the center of a square of foil.
- Top with equal portions of chopped carrots, potatoes and peppers.
- Season with dehydrated onions, Worcestershire sauce, salt and pepper to taste.
- Seal foil, checking for leaks. Place on hot coals for 10 to 15 minutes per side.

Buttermilk Biscuits

Ingredients
- 1/4 c shortening
- 1/4 t baking soda
- 2 c self-rising flour
- 3/4 c buttermilk

Directions
- Cut shortening into flour. Stir soda in milk and pour into flour and shortening. Stir until well blended.
- Pour out onto a floured surface and knead 12 to 15 times. Roll out and cut. Place on a <u>baking sheet</u> and bake at 450 degrees F. until brown.

Camp Au Gratin Potatoes

Ingredients
- 1 cn Corned Beef Or 2 Cans Tuna Or Similar
- Meat
- Boxes Au Gratin Potatoes
- c Water
- 1/2 c Dry Milk Powder
- 1/4 c Margarine Or Oil
- md Pot For Heating Water
- lg Pot For Potatoes
- Stirring Spoon

Directions
- Put the corned beef or tuna on the bottom of the pan. Open the potato packages and layer the potatoes on top of the meat.
- Sprinkle the cheese powder over the potatoes. Put the oil or margarine on the potatoes.
- Heat the water to near boiling and add the dry milk.
- Pour the hot liquid over the dry potatoes and put the pot on a moderate fire to simmer gently for 40 minutes. This arrangement should result in a slightly liquid mixture.
- Turn the pot from time to time if it is being
- kept at the edge of the fire to assure it heat all the way around.

- The oil or margarine is to keep the liquid from foaming. A smaller quantity or none can be used, but more care to keep the liquid from boiling over must be made.

Camp Chili

Ingredients

- 1 c Lentils
- 1 T Cumin
- T Tomato soup powder
- 1 t Oregano
- 2 T Masa (or Corn flour)
- 1 t Salt
- 1 T Chili Powder
- Clove Garlic
- 1 T Onion Flakes
- c Water

Directions

- Combine all the ingredients and simmer 30 - 45 Min.

Camp Cobbler Delight

Ingredients
- 1 cn Sliced peaches, large
- 1/4 lb Margarine
- 1 cn Fruit cocktail, large
- 1 c Brown sugar
- 1 cn Crushed pineapple, small
- 1 pk Cake mix
- 1/2 c tapioca, Instant

Directions
- In 12 inch foil lined <u>Dutch Oven</u>, combine fruit and tapioca.
- Sprinkle cake mix evenly over top of fruit. Sprinkle brown sugar over cake mix. Dab butter all over top of brown sugar.
- Place lid on oven. Bake 45 minutes to 1 hour. Use 6 to 8 coals on the bottom and 14 to 16 on the top. Cake is done when top is brown and cake has absorbed juices and is no longer dry.

Camp Hash

Ingredients
- c Shredded Hash Brown, Dried
- Taste
- Potatoes (Get At Costco)
- 1 lg Pot With A Lid
- 2 pk Onion Soup Mix
- 1 lg Spoon
- 1 1/2 lb Meat (Or Sausage),Ground
- c Water
- Assorted Seasonings

Directions
- Brown the meat in the bottom of the pan. Break up the meat as it cooks assuring that all the pink (raw) meat is cooked.
- Add the water and soup mix stirring to mix. Heat to boiling and simmer a few minutes. Add the dry potatoes and stir to mix.
- Cover the pot and move to the edge of the fire for about 10 minutes to allow the potatoes to swell up with the water.
- Move the pot back on the heat and stir while cooking the potatoes.
- Cook about 5-10 minutes. Serve hot.

- Seasonings may be added with the potatoes to the cooks taste. Hot peppers, chili powder, basil, Italian seasonings are good.

Camp Pasta

Ingredients

- lb Pasta -- any kind
- pk Spaghetti sauce mix
- 1 cn Tomato paste
- 1 lb Lean hamburger – ground turkey or
- Italian sausage

Directions

- Heat water to a boil in a large pot. In a smaller pot cook the meat and add the sauce mix, water, and tomato paste according to the instructions on the sauce package.
- Cook the pasta in the water for 8-10 minutes. Place the lid on the pot and with gloves or pot holders drain the water from the pasta through the crack between the lid and the pot.
- Putting the pot on a stump or log and letting the stump or log hold the weight of the pot helps.
- Mix the sauce with the drained pasta and serve.

Camp Potatoes

Ingredients

- Potatoes, sliced
- Onions, sliced
- T Butter or margarine
- 10 oz Cheddar cheese, sharp
- Salt & pepper to taste

Directions

- Grease a large square of heavy foil. Arrange sliced potatoes on foil, sprinkle with salt and pepper and cover with sliced onions.
- Add chunks of butter or margarine. Wrap and seal foil.
- Cook over hot coals on a grill until done (30 or 40 minutes depending on fire).
- Open foil and add thin-sliced cheddar strips.
- Cover again and grill for a couple of minutes, until cheddar melts.

Camp Stew

Ingredients

- lg Onions, cut up fine
- Twice as many squirrels as
- Butter beans
- chickens
- Corn
- pickled pork -or-,Slices
- Tomatoes
- bacon
- Red, black pepper & salt
- Irish potatoes

Directions

- Prepare one or more chickens, and twice as many squirrels, as for frying.
- Into the bottom of a pot or deep stew-pan, lay slices of pickled pork or bacon, cutting off the rind and rancid parts, if bacon is used.
- Put a layer of chicken, one of Irish potatoes peeled and sliced, two large onions cut up fine, butter beans, corn and tomatoes; red and black pepper and salt to taste; a layer of game, then of pork.
- Finish with a layer of vegetables; cover with water, and, putting on a well-fitting cover, set the vessel where the mixture will simmer gently and steadily for four hours.

Camper's Baked Potatoes

Ingredients

- Baking potatoes
- 1/4 t Garlic powder
- Onion, chopped
- 1/2 t Lemon pepper
- oz Green chiles
- Aluminum foil
- oz Black olives, chopped

Directions

- Scrub and chop baking potatoes into pieces, but do not peel.
- Prepare 6-8 square pieces of heavy-duty aluminum foil, one piece per serving. Place equal portions of the ingredients on each foil square.
- Fold the foil in a drug-store type fold, sealing ends.
- Place on barbecue grill for about 45-55 minutes.

Camper's Cookies

Ingredients

- c Flour
- 1 t Baking soda
- 1/2 t Salt
- 1/2 t Baking powder
- 1 c Margarine
- 1 c White sugar
- 1 c Brown sugar
- Eggs
- 1 t Vanilla
- 2 c Oats
- oz Semi-sweet chocolate chips
- 1 c Nuts

Directions

Sift together the flour, baking soda, salt, and baking powder.
Cream the margarine and the sugars together. Add the eggs and beat.
Add the flour mixture and mix well.
 Add the vanilla, oats, chocolate chips, and nuts.
Grease a 13x9x2 pan, and press mixture in evenly. Bake in a preheated oven 15 minutes at 350 F

Camper's Sausage

Ingredients

- 2 ½ kg Ground beef
- t Tender quick curing salt
- t Coarsely ground pepper
- t Garlic salt
- 2 t Mustard salt
- 1 t Hickory-smoked salt

Directions

- These will keep for several days without refrigeration.
- Mix together spices. Crumble meat and, with the hands, thoroughly mix in spices.
- Cover and refrigerate for 24 hours. Mix again and refrigerate another 24 hours.
- On the third day, shape into five rolls about 38 mm in diameter. Place 50 mm apart on a metal rack and bake at 150 degrees F (65 degrees C) for 8 hours, turning every 2 hours.

Camper's Stew

Ingredients

- 1 cn Whole new potatoes
- 1 cn Meatballs with gravy
- 1 cn Green beans
- oz Can tomato sauce
- 1 cn carrots, Diced
- T onion, Dehydrated

Directions

- Drain liquid from vegetables, save 1 cup.
- Combine all ingredients, bring to a boil and serve.

Campers Hobo Pie

Ingredients

- 1 lb Ground beef
- Carrots sliced
- Potatoes cubed
- md Onion, sliced in 1/4" pieces
- Butter

Directions

- Form hamburger patties and put one patty, with individual of whole carrots, sliced potatoes and sliced onions, on a sheet of aluminum foil.
- Brush everything with butter and sprinkle with salt and pepper.
- Fold foil over food and place on charcoal or open fire
- Cook for an hour, turning every 15 minutes. Chicken can be substituted for the hamburger meat.

Campers Pizza Pie

Ingredients
- oz pizza or spaghetti sauce
- 1 lb Wheat bread
- ¼ lb Mozzarella cheese
- Pepperoni

Directions
- Using the pie iron, take two slices of bread, put 1 ½ tablespoons pizza sauce on one slice of bread.
- Top with Mozzarella cheese and sliced pepperoni.
- Place other side of bread on top and butter outer sides of bread.
- Put sandwich into pie iron and place in coals of fire.
- Cook until bread is toasted.

Campfire Biscuits

Ingredients

- c Jiffy Baking mix
- 2/3 c Water

Directions

- Mix well and knead. If too soft, add a little more mix
- for a dry handling dough.
- Put flour on aluminum foil and pat dough to about ½ inch thickness. Cut into biscuits.
- Bake at moderate heat for 15-20 minutes, or until biscuits are lightly browned on top.
- Remove from heat and serve hot.

Campfire Cinnamon Coffeecake

Ingredients

- T Butter or margarine
- 1 c Packaged biscuit mix
- 1/3 c Evaporated milk, undiluted
- 1 T Prepared cinnamon-sugar

Directions

- Make Coffeecake: Cut butter into tiny pieces over biscuit mix in medium bowl.
- Toss lightly with fork until butter is coated. Make a well in center.
- Pour in milk and cinnamon-sugar, stirring with fork just until mixture is moistened.
- Turn dough into a lightly greased and floured 8-inch shiny, heavy skillet.
- With floured hands, pat down evenly into the skillet.
- Cook, covered, over very low heat, 12 to 15 minutes, or until a <u>cake tester</u> or wooden pick inserted in center comes out clean.
- For Topping: Spread the coffeecake with 2 Ts butter or margarine. Then sprinkle 1 teaspoon prepared cinnamon-sugar over all of it.
- Cut into quarters, and serve warm.

Campfire Fondue

Ingredients
- c Cheddar, Shredded OR swiss cheese
- T All purpose flour
- 1/4 t Paprika
- 1 cn Cream of celery soup
- 1/2 c Beer (or white wine or -water)

Directions
- Toss together, cheese, flour and paprika. Combine soup and beer.
- Heat. Over low heat add cheese, stirring until completely melted.
- Serve with French Bread Cubes

Campfire Fried Rice

Ingredients
- pk Precooked rice (7 oz)
- c Boiling water
- 1 cn Spam luncheon meat - (7 oz) diced
- Envelope fried rice seasoning mix (1 oz)

Directions
- Place rice in small bowl; pour boiling water over. Cover and let stand 5 minutes.
- Fluff with a fork. Mix in Spam and seasoning mix.
- Transfer mixture to medium skillet.
- Cook over medium heat 5 minutes, stirring often.

Campfire Hash

Ingredients

- TB cooking oil
- 1 lg onion chopped
- garlic cloves minced
- lg potatoes -- peeled and cubed
- 1 lb smoked sausage -- cubed
- 1 cn chopped green chiles (4 oz)
- 1 cn whole kernel corn drained

Directions

- In a <u>Dutch oven</u>, heat oil. Sauté onion and garlic until tender.
- Add potatoes. Cook, uncovered, over medium heat for 20 minutes, stirring occasionally.
- Add sausage; cook and stir until potatoes are tender and well browned, about 10 minutes more.
- Stir in chilies and corn; cook until heated through.

Campfire Pork And Beans

Ingredients

- Bacon slices, cut 1 1/2 "
- 1/2 c Chopped onion
- 1/2 c Chopped green bell pepper
- 53 oz Can pork and beans
- 1/4 c Molasses
- 1/4 t Tabasco sauce

Directions

- Heat oven to 375 degrees. Fry bacon until crisp. Set aside.
- Reserve 2 tablespoons drippings in pan. Sauté onion and green pepper in drippings until tender.
- Combine beans, molasses and red pepper sauce in a 2 ½ quart casserole.
- Bake 40 to 45 minutes. Top with bacon.

Dutch Oven Biscuits

Ingredients

- 2 c Flour
- 4 T Solid shortening
- 1/2 t Salt
- 1 c Milk (diluted ok), Canned
- 3 t Baking powder

Directions

- Blend flour, salt, baking powder and mash in shortening with a fork until crumbly. Add milk and stir until the dough sags down into trough left by spoon as it moves around the bowl.
- Turn dough out on a floured surface, knead for 30 seconds, pat out gently until it is 1/2 inch thick. Cut with a round cutter or pinch off pieces of dough and form by hand.
- Put biscuits into a greased Dutch Oven, cover, and bury in bright coals for 5 or 10 minutes or until golden brown.

Dutch Oven Trout

Ingredients

- 6   8 inch trout
- 1 t ground pepper
- 12 sl Bacon

Directions

- Filet the trout. Lay three slices of bacon on the bottom of a Dutch
- Oven, put 1/2 a trout, flesh-side-down, on each slice.
- Sprinkle pepper lightly over upper sides of fish. Arrange a second layer of bacon and fish at right angles to the first, and continue to arrange other layers, each at right angles to one below it, until all the fish halves are in the pot.
- Cover the Dutch Oven, bury in coals, cook 35-40 minutes. Serve a slice of bacon with each half-fish. If you cook bass this way, skin them first.

Flank Steak Teriyaki

Ingredients

- 4 - 6 flank steaks
- 1 T Salad oil
- 1/4 c Sugar
- 1 t Ginger
- 1/2 t MSG
- 4 - 6 pineapple slices
- 1/2 c Soy sauce
- 2 T Sherry (optional)
- 1 ea garlic, crushed

Directions

- To form marinade, combine all except steaks and pineapple.
- Mix well and pour over steaks. Let marinate 1 to 1-1/2 hours.
- Fry steaks in very hot oven or skillet brushing once with marinade. Add pineapple during last few minutes, brush with marinade and cover.
- Cook 3-5 min. Serve over rice.

Foiled Burgers Aka "Jack Special"

Ingredients

- 1 lb beef, Ground
- 4   Squares heavy duty foil . (16x16 inches)
- 4   Carrots, chopped
- 1 cn New potatoes, sliced (16oz)
- 2 sm Green peppers, chopped
- onion flakes, Dehydrated
- Worcestershire sauce
- Salt & pepper, To Taste

Directions

- Separate the meat into 4 portions. Place each portion in the center of a aluminum foil square.
- Top with equal portions of chopped carrots, potatoes and bell peppers.
- Season with dehydrated onion flakes, Worcestershire sauce, salt and/or pepper to suit your taste.
- Seal the foil, check for leaks. Place on the coals for 10 to 15
  minutes per side.

Great Outdoors Potatoes

Ingredients

- 6   Potatoes
- 1/2 t pepper, Fresh Ground
- 1/4 c Olive oil
- 1 t onion, Minced
- 2 t Lemon juice
- Pureed garlic clove
- 1 t Dijon mustard
- 1 t Paprika
- 1/2 t Corriander

Directions

- Scrub potatoes and cut into quarters, keeping skins on.
- Boil until tender, and coat them with the dressing which you can prepare in advance.
- Wrap the potato quarters in tin foil, and place on coal to brown. Delicious with meat or fish.

Grilled Sausage & Sweet Mustard In Tortillas

Ingredients

- 1 lb Hot or sweet Italian -sausage or -Spanish choriza*
- 1 c Hearty red wine (such as –Italian -Barolo or Spanish R10ia)
- 9   8-inch flour or 6-inch corn -tortillas
- Honey mustard or Dijon -mustard

Directions

- Place sausage in single layer in 9-inch skillet. Pour wine over sausage.
- Bring to boil. Reduce heat, cover partially and simmer until sausages are cooked through, turning frequently, about 12 minutes.
- Remove sausage from pan and cool slightly. Discard liquid. (Can be prepared 1 day ahead.
- Cover tightly and refrigerate. Bring to room temperature before continuing.)
- Prepare barbecue (medium-high heat).
- Cut sausages into 1/2-inch slices. Thread slices on long metal skewers, using 3 to 4 skewers.
- Cut tortillas into quarters and wrap in foil. Place tortillas on side of grill to heat through.
- Grill sausage until heated through and charred on all sides, about 5 minutes.

- Remove sausage from skewers and place in serving bowl.
- Serve sausage with tortillas and mustard.

*A fresh pork link sausage flavored with garlic and spices, and milder than Mexican chorizo. Spanish chorizo is available at Spanish markets.

Homemade Granola

Ingredients

- 4 c Rolled oats
- 1/4 c Sesame Seeds
- 2 T Light Sesame oil
- 1 t Ground Cinnamon
- 1/2 c Wheat Germ
- 1/4 c Shelled Peanuts (or soybeans
- 1/4 c Honey
- 1/2 t Grated Nutmeg or Cardamon
- Raisins, grated coconut, nuts, or dried fruit

Directions

- Preheat the oven to 350 deg F. Toast the oats, wheat germ, seeds, and legumes lightly on a baking sheet for 5-10 minutes, until slightly browned.
- Remove and cool. Heat the honey and oil together in a small pan; drizzle it over the dry mixture.
- Sprinkle with cinnamon or cardomon. Return the mixture to the baking sheet and heat in the oven for 5 minutes.
- Stir or turn. Bake for a few minutes more, until crispy but not too browned.
- Remove and cool. Add raisins, nuts, or dried fruit if desired.

Irish Soda Bread

Ingredients

- 2 1/2 c Milk
- 1/2 c Rolled oats
- 2 T White vinegar
- 1 t Baking soda
- 4 c Whole wheat flour
- 2 t Salt
- 1 c All-purpose white flour

Directions

- Preheat the oven to 375F, or preheat the dutch oven, top and bottom.
- Put the milk in a small bowl. Stir in the vinegar and mix to make the milk sour; set aside. In a large mixing bowl, mix together the whole wheat flour, white flour, oats, baking soda, and salt.
- Add the soured mixture to the flour mixture and stir until all the dry ingredients are moistened.
- Place the dough on a floured board and lightly knead about ten times, until the dough is smooth.
- Form the dough into a 9-inch round loaf, place it on a cookie sheet or in a preheated dutch oven, and with a sharp knife, mark the top of the loaf with an X, cutting the dough about 1/8 inch deep.
- Bake for 50 to 60 minutes, or until the bread is brown and sounds hollow when tapped.

- Cool and serve.

Lazy Or "Dump" Cobbler

Ingredients
- 12-inch Dutch oven
- 25 charcoal briquettes (15
- -on bottom,10 on top)
- 2 cn peaches with syrup, Sliced
- -(29-30 oz. cans)
- 1 pk Cake mix (white, yellow or
- -spiced)
- 1/3   Stick margarine
- cinnamon to taste, Ground

Directions
- Place oven over hot bottom briquettes. Pour contents of peach cans into oven.
- Spread dry cake mix evenly over peaches (eggs or shortening not needed!) Sprinkle cinnamon over all to taste.
- Cut margarine into equal slices and place in checkerboard pattern on top.
- Put lid on top of oven. Add hot briquettes and bake for about 45 minutes or until done. This recipe will have a layer of peaches with a cake covering that the boiling syrup self mixes. If mixing the cake in with the peaches is preferred, about 1/2 way

through baking, mix everything together and continue baking until done. Spoon out cobbler into bowls, add milk or ice cream.

Mountain Man Breakfast

Ingredients

- 12-inch Dutch oven
- 1 md Onion, chopped
- 1/2 lb Bacon, cut into small pieces
- 1 pk 32-oz. hash brown potatoes
- 12   Eggs
- 1 1/2 lb Cheddar cheese, grated
- 8-oz. jar of salsa

Directions

- Preheat Dutch oven over 10 charcoal briquettes and preheat lid with 14 briquettes.
- Brown 1/2 pound bacon. Add onion and cook until clear.
- Remove bacon and onions from Dutch oven and drain on paper towels.
- Wipe excess grease out of dutch oven and place back over hot briquettes.
- Stir in the 32-ounce bag of hash brown potatoes.

- Fry until potatoes are golden brown, then mix the bacon and onions back in.
- Break 12 eggs into medium mixing bowl and beat thoroughly. Pour over potatoes, bacon and onions. Cover with hot lid and cook until eggs are almost solid.

- Sprinkle with 1 1/2 pounds grated cheddar cheese.
- Continue cooking until eggs set and cheese melts. Just before serving, top with 1 8-oz jar of hot, medium, or mild salsa, according to taste.

Never Fail Dumplings

Ingredients

- 3 t Baking Powder
- 6 T Cold water
- 1 c Flour
- 1 T Oil
- 1 md Egg
- 1 t Salt

Directions

- Beat the egg well then add the 6T of cold water. Measure the water carefully. Add the oil and salt and whisk together.
- Mix the baking powder and flour together. Blend the two mixes into a smooth batter quickly.
- Drop into boiling stew and cover continuing to boil for 15- 20 mins.
- Try to resist the urge to peek too often - the dumplings will rise and produce a light tender crust - a cold draft will cause them to fall. They can also be served as a dessert by cooking in boiling water and served with pancake syrup or jam drizzled over them.

Onioned Potatoes

Ingredients

- 6 md Baking potatoes
- 1 pk Envelope dry onion soup mix
- 1/2 c Soft butter (or margarine)

Directions

- Scrub potatoes but do not pare. Cut each in three or four
lengthwise slices.
- Blend butter and soup mix; spread on slices. Reassemble the potatoes.
- Wrap each potato in square of foil, overlapping ends. Bake until tender, turning once.
- Takes 45 to 60 minutes on the grill or right on top of coals depending on size of potatoes.

www.ingramcontent.com/pod-product-compliance
Lightning Source LLC
Chambersburg PA
CBHW071444070526
44578CB00001B/208